India

Another Way of Life

India

Another Way of Life

Tzannis Tzannetakis

Translated by
Alexandra Doumas

D.K. Printworld (P) Ltd.
NEW DELHI-110015

Cataloging in Publication Data – DK

Tzannetakis, Tzannis.
India : another way of life.

1. India – Description and travel. I. Title.

ISBN 81-246-0083-X

First Published in India in 1998

Photographs by:
Ms. A. B. and Printworld's Collection

Published by:

D.K. Printworld (P) Ltd.
Regd. office: '*Sri Kunj*', F-52, Bali Nagar
New Delhi - 110 015
Phones: (011) 545-3975; 546-6019; *Fax:* (011) 546-5926
E-mail: dkprint@4mis.com

Printed by: DP's Impressive Impressions, New Delhi - 110059

Then said Maitreyī: "If, indeed, Venerable Sir, this whole earth filled with wealth were mine, would I be immortal through that?" "No", said Yajñavalkya: "Like the life of the rich even so would your life be. Of immortality, however, there is no hope through wealth."

—***Bṛhadāraṇyaka Upaniṣad***, Fourth Brāhmaṇa
(The conversation of Yajñavalkya and maitreyī
on the absolute self)

Foreword

India like Greece is the cradle of one of the world's oldest civilisations. Many traditions extant in India today have their origins, in customs and beliefs that go back five thousand years. Over the centuries, India has been viewed by people outside its boundaries as a land of splendour, richness, vision and effervescent ideas. Like a magnet it has attracted the attention of diverse nations from the very beginning of history.

Fearsome conquerors, itinerant mendicants, artists and monks have wandered across the mountain fastness that bounds the northern borders, to drink deep of the civilization of this ancient land. It was romance, adventure and often greed which motivated travellers like these from all nations to undertake the journey to India. From China, Arabia and beyond they came. They met Indian kings and travelled through their kingdoms. They were struck by the variegated hues of Indian society. They were awed by its artistic achievements and religious values and delighted by its contented and colourful people. Hiuen-Tsang, Fa-hsien, I-Tsing, Al-Beruni, Ibu Battuta, Nicolo dei Conti, Barbosa Duarte and last but not least, Alexander the Great are amongst those who travelled through India with their eyes wide open and their pens in their hands. It is these travellers and their companions who have immortalized the country in its various stages of flowering, through their brilliant writings. They fell in love with India and in turn were honoured and loved by this land.

Tzannis Tzannetakis, a former Greek Prime Minister who made an informal visit to India as a traveller a few years ago is no stranger to our country. Over 30 years ago, long before he had touched the shores of the Indian peninsula, he undertook a monumental task by translating India's spiritual and philosophical fount of wisdom, the Upanishads into Greek. That at such a young age Mr. Tzannetakis was able to grapple with and absorb the meaning of the Upanishads, the highest repository of Indian philosophy, speaks highly of his sharp intellect and his keen sensitivity to foreign cultural traditions. Tzannetakis' interest in India has now led to another fascinating book "India Another Way of Life", in which Tzannetakis' experiences in India are vividly recounted.

It is not often that we are privileged to read travel books written by persons as distinguished as the erstwhile Prime Minister, but 'India Another Way of Life' is really much more than a travelogue. Reading through its pages one can clearly see the eyes of an artist, listen to the ears of a musician and feel the sensibility of a poet and the spirit of a wise sage deeply steeped in the Hellenic civilisation.

Mr. Tzannetakis' work transports the reader, almost physically to the scenes, sights and smells being described. Mr. Tzannetakis' account is admirable because his extraordinary sensitivity to the cultural traditions of multi-lingual and multi-ethnic and multi-religions India comes through clearly. Mr. Tzannetakis takes us on a journey through some of our more ancient and romantic places: Rajasthan, where ochre forts straddle the land and camels with colourfully dressed people roam at a pace which blends unmistakably with the barren yet gentle desert landscape. He shows us the holy city of Banaras which like Athens is one of the oldest urban centres in the world. His descriptions of forts, palaces and monuments such as that indescribable favourite the Taj Mahal, are a treat to read.

In admiring the 20th century and India's march towards progress the writer focuses on two great Indians who have contributed so much to the making of modern India. A chapter on Mahatma Gandhi and Jawaharlal Nehru recognises these two remarkable men as the architects of modern India; each of them in his own inimitable way moulded the history of our country and left an indelible impact on the world as we know it today. This splendid volume written first in Greek by Mr. Tzannetakis has already made a successful appearance in that language. Thanks to the ICCR, the English version of Mr. Tzannetakis' book is being published now. This is a commendable effort for it ensures that a much wider audience is privileged to savour and enjoy the many delights that this charming book has to offer.

Aftab Seth
Ambassador of India to Greece
1992-1996

Contents

Introduction

A journey to India is something different. It is quite unlike a journey to any other land, that may give you some experience of its culture or its misery. It is a journey that is bound to transform you, one way or another. It will force you to penetrate the tragedy unfolding daily in that vast country. An endless interplay between the admirable and the abhorrent.

A journey to India is not always easy. It is not for everyone. It is not for those, mainly Westerners, who are used to judging another country on the basis of the dry, technocratic indices of consumerism they have adopted to measure their own performance – how many washing machines, telephones, motor cars, televisions, videos are there per caput.

Whoever visits India imbued with Western concepts of civilisation and progress is certain to find an under-developed country with very serious problems. More than likely, he will take the next plane home, or head for some other destination that will guarantee him those comforts he has grown up with, that determine his attitudes. In India the tap water is undrinkable, raw vegetables are a health hazard, the seething mass of humanity is unbearable and the air is filled with the odours of jostling men and animals – which wander freely in the streets. The means of transport are rare, primitive, infrequent. In general, all the conveniences of everyday life are limited and fraught with problems.

On the contrary, for travellers with an open mind, eager to see and to seek a different civilisation, India offers amazing possibilities for speculation, hitherto unimagined. It enriches them with values at once timeless and timely.

With the vastness and variety of its terrain and cultures, India, for all the improvements in its communications, only permits the traveller to visit – and even less get to know – a tiny part of the immense country.

Walled to the north by the mountain massifs of the Himalayas where the two great rivers, the Indus and the Ganga, rise, the country unfolds over a distance of 3,200 kilometres – covered by deserts, jungles, forests, fields and plains, stretching from Myanmar and China to as far as Pakistan, from the border with Tibet to the hot southern tip of Cape Comorin.

The peoples who came in waves from the North and the North-West at various times, pushing through the mountain passes in order to conquer and to settle the land, created a multifarious society in a state larger in size than the European Union. To its old inhabitants, the Dravidians, were added Aryan invaders from Central Asia, who created a new world. Then followed the Greeks, the Muslims, and lastly, the European colonialists – the Portuguese, Dutch, French and British, who remained in the country until its independence in 1947. Then began the rebuilding of a new India, divided into twenty-five states and six Union Territories. This new India holds within it a pot-pourri of the peoples who passed through it, an amalgam which is forged into something different, into another outlook on life that struggles to preserve and to transmit to all a new system of values and ideas.

India today lives diachronically. It lives simultaneously in different centuries. Here, an advanced modern society with a significant industry coexists harmoniously with primitive tribes and millions of paupers, wretched and without hope. But between the ancient and the modern, the wealth and the poverty, there is the apotheosis of humaneness – of a humaneness created and established over thousands of years of Indian history, through its religion and its civilisation. A civilisation which spread and conquered virtually the whole of eastern Asia. A civilisation whose central axis is non-violence, which accepts and respects, beyond what the majority believes, all religions and life-styles which coexist in concord in society. India is the country which assimilates everything that is good, and is in constant flux.

One of the elements of the Indian civilisation that surprises the Western visitor and contradicts acutely his own cultural experience is the 'Caste System' – the hierarchical stratification of society into groups.

The division of men into castes is a system born of the dominant religion of the Indians, Hinduism, thousands of years ago under the pressure of the tribes, social groups and the large population of the country. The caste system has been intensely criticised by the West. In a land of hundreds of millions, in a society with enormous contrasts and the danger of chaos always lurking, as in India, the caste system conceals its own practical usefulness. The castes give men an identity, the knowledge of where they stand socially and how they must live. They provide security and define the diet, the rituals and even the choice of a spouse. When the castes were created there were four. Today, however, they have proliferated to over three thousand, covering an enormous spectrum which begins with the brahmins and ends with the untouchables.

Caste is an all-powerful element in Indian life. Although it originated in Hinduism, it has nowadays infiltrated the communities of Muslims, Sikhs and Christians, which theoretically lie outside this system. It is a force for stability, strong and conservative, a defence against racial discrimination, which in our age has been internationally condemned and is tending to disappear. But this system gives rise to continual struggles in India, mainly by the Harijans – a caste of the untouchables so named by Mahatma Gandhi, the 'Father of the Nation' – who strive politically for vindication, claiming their rights. This, however, does not prevent the castes from continuing to play their important role in the political life of the modern Indian republic, since the fabric of India's strength has been woven with the ideas and life of the Hindus, such as man's reincarnation and predestination.

There is an old oriental maxim that says: 'happiness is the distance between what you desire and what you have'. The smaller that distance, the closer you are to happiness.

We, in the West, in our ranking of values, have placed money and power at the top of the scale. We have been transformed into a consumer society, unleashing, via technology, powers and dynamics which we ourselves cannot control. We are caught up in a vicious circle, that we entered happy and unsuspecting, without knowing whether there was any way out. The ideal for the Western man is the acquisition of more and more goods – which he does not necessarily need. It gives him social prestige and relieves him of tiring tasks. However, in the course of acquiring more and more material possessions, man becomes inevitably enslaved to that system which provides him the necessary money. At the same time, even more needs are created, entailing a new struggle to fulfil them. A circle with no beginning and no end . . . without the contentment of the mountaineer who reaches the summit and sits down to rest, surveying the view that is the reward for his conquest . . . since a new target appears even before the previous one has been met. A chain which shackles and numbs thought, and transforms men into instruments without volition, without joy and certainly without dreams – the foundation stones of the struggles that elevate human nature.

India lives in a world of its own. A world traced out by its religion thousands of years ago. A world which liberates man's thought to concentrate on the essence and not the phenomena of life. So the Indians espouse a clear set of values, such as self-control, maturity, lack of jealousy, lack of unbridled ambition, creativity, love, self-denial and courage. There is also the realisation that we live in this world together with all animate creatures, those that spend their life as insignificant little units. Thus the Indians try to improve their selves by setting logical and not impossible goals, with the dominant sentiment being love and respect of one's neighbour. It is this feeling which makes the Indians receptive to all ways of thinking and all ways of life.

India is the largest democratic society in the world. Democracy here is not a dead letter. It is a vital rule, manifest in all the functions of familial, social and national life.

After Independence in 1947, India, this continent-state, endowed with a very ancient history whose roots go back five thousand years, had to mark out its future course with inhabitants of different creeds, races and traditions in order to live together in concord and work together to rebuild the new state. The differences between the inhabitants of Kashmir, Punjab, Maharashtra, Kerala are analogous to differences between the Swedes, Portuguese, Belgians and Greeks in Europe. In 1947 the population of India was 350 million; today it has reached more than 850 million, increasing at an average rate of about ten million every year. It is forecast that by the beginning of the next century its population will exceed that of China, and India will be the most populous country in the world.

This population explosion creates tremendous problems for the political leadership. And these are not only problems of nutrition. In every society with rising expectations demands are created for a higher level of education, better health care, more jobs and adequate housing. These demands are transformed into political pressures.

India can be proud of the progress it has made in recent years. Improvements in the sector of health and the control of epidemics are one of the reasons for the rise in population. The years when India was short of food and obliged to import cereals are now past. India has learnt to feed its growing millions, thanks to its agricultural revolution, which directed investments into healthier crops and improved the irrigation system. The people, it is abundantly clear, are better dressed, better nourished, better educated and better housed. Large sections of Indian society are developing. The privatisation and liberalisation policies followed today, together with international cooperation, affirm that India will be able to exploit its immense resources. The Indian nation can be proud of the path it is taking. It is, however, impossible to ignore the ubiquitous poverty and the hungry millions.

• • •

With all these thoughts in mind, I decided to visit India, a country whose philosophy had fascinated me when, many years ago, I like many others had tried to seek the meaning of life. Then I had read texts which have left a deep impression on my mind regarding inquiries into a better life, one adapted to man – the dominant, the unique, the one – who since the time of his appearance on the planet has tried and still tries to answer the basic questions life inexorably poses.

So I too had entered the world of Indian philosophy. In the Indian texts I had encountered the same questions as those posed by Thales, Pythagoras and Socrates. In addition to the *Vedas*, I had studied the *Upanishads*, which are the very dawn of Indian philosophy and religion, and I had translated some of these into Greek and published them several years ago.

This journey to India was not a tourist's trip. In the company of a few friends I tried to look for and look into those traits, wherever they existed, that contributed to India's efforts to follow another way of life. Our itinerary did not cover the whole of this enormous country, but only a few characteristic parts of it; the visit to these places, however, impelled me to write down my thoughts on the past, the present and the future of India, with the eye of a man charmed by the course of these people and who hopes their endeavour to chart another way of life will bear fruit. An endeavour which does not just concern India. It concerns the whole world, not least my own homeland, Greece. A country which too has a very ancient civilisation and which is, I feel, at a crossroads similar in many ways to the situation in India.

Bombay

The Gateway to India

When you travel eastwards you feel night is endless, for the globe on which we live revolves in the same direction as the movement of the aeroplane.

Above the clouds, sitting in the window seat, gazing down at the vast sea of white spread out below, you try to recall what you once read and revered . . . . years ago now . . . Then, when you were looking for the truth in prophets and laws. It is the final preparation for the great journey you have planned, carefully, full of anxiety and trepidation . . . like the first meeting with a loved one you have not met, of whom you have only heard garbled opinions . . . opinions in which you distinguish . . . regardless of the outer casing . . . a strong, clear, primordial kernel which scorns the husk and pushes inside to the essence of life, breaking the chains which, like the spider's web, men let wind around them.

Deep in your thoughts, you are unaware of the change, which is quicker than thought . . . the rudeness of technology allows no time for you to feel the emotion passing slowly through your body, rising up with the blood into the heart and mind. It flings you abruptly into other worlds,

← *The Gateway to India in Bombay*

←↑*Washermen toil in an outdoor laundry, while clothes dry in the sun*

without introduction – as if you were thrown from a ship into the chilly sea in the month of March. Then you are forced to concentrate your being on a single point, forgetting the years you have lived and what you gained in them, moment by moment, day by day . . . with your senses always on the alert. You feel you should be born again in order to comprehend, without prejudice, another world now opening up before you. The bump of the aeroplane's wheels – with the landing, daybreak now – brings you here, to another land, to another world. Bombay.

Your first contact with Indian soil is astonishing. A succession of feelings, alternating with people, buildings, odours, sounds, mercilessly pounds your senses. So much so that you are unable to think . . . you just remain dumbstruck, staring around you . . . at the human ants . . . scrimmaging to take their luggage from the badly-worn conveyor belts at the Santa Cruz airport in Bombay (now, Mumbai). Suitcases and colourful bundles, inventively tied to secure the belongings. We gazed astonished at the human tide overflowing everywhere, clambering, shoving, drawing back to surge again, to pull the other piece of its life . . . and to drag along with it anything at hand. So we too, we know not how, found ourselves out in the streets, a morsel of the mass moving between stones, mud and wood . . . all shrouded in the morning mist.

This was our first contact with the country. Hard, you could say inhuman, for people like us who are able to spend far more than we need . . . On the way from the airport to the hotel we saw deprivation and poverty at its extreme . . . far worse than you could possibly imagine. Human spectres all around awoke in us a sense of guilt – our guilt, the guilt of those we

← *The Taj Hotel, one of Bombay's most characteristic buildings*

represent, willingly or unwillingly, the guilt of us all who left our fellow men unaided to reach this point, while we chase the pursuits of refined leisure, losing the sense of the simple and the lovely.

India is a land of stark contrasts which seem reconciled and which alternate unexpectedly. So it was that another aspect of the city presented itself to us a few hours later, when we were wandering through its neighbourhoods. We crossed the broad, coastal avenue that skirts the gulf with the island at its southern tip, on which Bombay is built. Next to the avenue is an enormous beach – Chowpathi Square – a venue for assemblies and feasts. At sunset the sand is filled with people from all over the city, who come here to spend a few hours by the sea and enjoy the changing colours on the horizon as the sun sinks into the ocean.

The avenue leads to the Malabar Hills, the aristocratic suburb of Bombay, the only sparsely populated part of the city . . . its opulent villas surrounded by gardens with lush vegetation. Here are the 'Hanging Gardens' and the Nehru Park, a beautifully designed park in which human

← *Chhatarpati Shivaji (Victoria) Terminal,*

care and love transforms nature into colourful works of art. Plants are clipped in the shape of animals, flower beds remind you of canvases by modern painters . . . and between them branch well-paved pathways with benches set under shady trees, to make your stroll more comfortable and pleasant.

Nariman Point

A little beyond are the famous 'Towers of Silence', the cemetery of the Parsees. A park cut off from the outside world by a towering wall. Not even the relatives of the dead are allowed to go beyond a certain point. They remain in the park and pray. Special porters carry the dead to the top of the cylindrical towers . . . carrion for the vultures hovering expectantly in the sky. Within a few minutes the corpses are stripped of all flesh. The bones are cast into wells, to turn into dust with the passage of time.

There are two explanations for this strange method of 'burial'. According to one, the Zoroastrian religion – the Parsees are its last surviving community, numbering less than one hundred thousand believers – respects earth and fire to the extent that it will not defile them with the bodies of the dead. According to the other, rich and poor are thus united in death.

The Parsees are descendants of Persian

immigrants who came here 1300 years ago. Persecuted in their homeland by the Muslims, they settled in the wider area of west-central India. With the development of Bombay they gathered here, where they now constitute a small minority of its population. All are wealthy, educated and highly influential in the life of the city and of India as a whole. They control building activity, industry, commerce, and are renowned for their business acumen and charitable works.

Children frolic in the water

We visited the Gateway to India, an arch at the edge of a large square near the waterfront, not far from the harbour. An arch which symbolically welcomes all those who arrive in India by sea, since Bombay is one of the country's largest ports.

We scrutinised the countless volumes neatly arranged on the shelves of the Bombay Central Library, a Neoclassical building with Doric columns, and were surprised at the Indians' habit of coming to the library .... to read the newspapers. Scores of Indians in their white garb, sitting round tables or lounging in armchairs ... devour every last item of news crammed into the many pages.

A little farther off the market place offers the visitor not only the chance to buy delicious fruit, spices and whatever else you can imagine, but also a joyous symphony of colours and forms presented by the piles of oranges, apples, mangoes and all

A fountain in the city centre

types of vegetables, combined with the presence of the white-clad traders . . . and the colourful dress – the *saris* – of the women.

That evening we were guests at the home of a Parsee family in Malabar, the most beautiful part of Bombay. Clever, cultured people. We conversed simply, calmly . . . a discussion for the purpose of bringing people close together. We exchanged our experiences, without ulterior motives, without insinuations. We listened to their thoughts on the present and the future of this country, enjoying the conversation which was accompanied by a light meal, and experienced what is to be rarely found in similar social intercourse in Greece. And all this in a humane environment, with candlelight . . . flowers . . . little statues placed inside and outside the house . . . January in Bombay . . . since their abode, the house and garden, is a single space. You come across such a humane atmosphere often in India. It is an approach to life rid of the excesses that abound in the West. It is a course through the essential elements of life, where austerity dominates, enhancing the beauty which nature itself lends. Time passed without us realising it.

• • •

On our second stay in Bombay, we saw a different side of it. We felt the pulse of the big city struggling to survive and take shape in the living conditions imposed by modern technology, matching the legacy of the colonial period with a new dynamism born of the independent, free state. Alongside the impressive Victorian edifices erected here by the British, faithful to the models of the metropolis, in what is now Bombay's administrative core – with the railway station, commissioner's headquarters, colleges, banks, hotels – rise more recent buildings covering the city's other needs. Bombay is suffocating from population explosion, its inhabitants multiplying each year.

But behind the lay-out of the city lie complex problems of social stratification.

Before Independence, the ruling class was made up of the British and a few Indians, who had the requisite education, income and knowledge, who were able to create jobs and earn money to ensure a comfortable life. There was this elite and the masses, the people, who struggled to survive mostly in wretched circumstances.

After Independence, the ruling class was replaced by those of the British who stayed on together with various other non-nationals – who happened to be here, without homeland. They make plenty of money and live 'like lords', in a city that is foreign to them. Their only links with Bombay are their long-standing residence, force of habit and affluence, which they are by no means willing to relinquish, as well as the fact that they have no other home to settle in since they are uprooted from their countries of origin.

So they get rich here. They run and frequent clubs with habits alien to the place. They swap wives, buying and selling, for their sole aim in life is to have a good time, so alien in mentality to Indian philosophy and the civilisation which germinated and took root in this land.

These were my thoughts as I left the Cricket Club of India (CCI) in Bombay, conscious yet again of the stark contrasts one meets with everyday in this country. And the conviction began to take hold in me . . . that all these are temporary . . . because India has begun to find its way, to organise its society and to participate in the international community in its own dynamic manner.

Before we left Bombay we visited the house of Gandhi, which has been turned into a museum with collections of books and objects that were the companions of this great Indian leader. Dozens of sculpted representations of important milestones in Gandhi's life complete the picture of this extraordinary man – an exemplar for the Indians – whose humility, faith and vision have left their stamp on the history of modern India.

Ajanta-Ellora
Art Infused with Life

Travelling northeast of Bombay, on the large Deccan Plateau that covers the central part of the great Indian peninsula, you leave behind the city with its noise, its bustle and its marked contrasts.

You are now transported to a land where life rolls along calmly, with its minor problems, tardy as the carts drawn by the buffalo with their coloured horns. Red, yellow and, above all, the Indian's favourite colour, blue on the horns are in keeping with the colours of the *saris* of the women and the white costumes of the men sitting in the carts.

Aurangabad, the city that lives in another age, another world. In a world without worries, concerned only with small and humble things . . . work, what to wear, what to eat, waking up the next day to repeat the same . . . in the streets with the huts, the animals, the children and the crowds. And yet you feel something new is being born, something that is trying shyly but steadily to change the way of life.

Here, close to the poverty towers a smart new building, the city's law court. Beyond is a bank and a little beyond that, a really beautiful hotel, where we stayed while we were in Aurangabad. A building of Mughal-Arabian architecture set in the midst of enormous well-planned gardens with trees, bushes, lawns and water, and furnishing all the comforts a traveller could desire. Comforts not easily found in modern hotels in the Western world. You feel you have suddenly woken up in another world, a world you were dreaming of . . . far from the barbarity of our own, a barbarity imposed by technology.

And we return to the dream, the dream of the boy we met entering a mosque – we had stopped in its garden for a while – who came up to us, foreigners, to talk to us and to learn about the outside world – for him so remote – that we represented.

Living as he did, close to nature, surrounded by flowers and trees, he had decided to become a botanist in order to offer something better to his land, following the things he had learnt from his parents and the milieu in which he had grown up.

The city of Aurangabad was built next to a village in 1610 and was made the capital in 1635 by Aurangzeb, one of the rulers of the Muslim Mughal dynasty. Today it is a regional centre of culture and history, with some of the best colleges and universities in Maharashtra state.

• • •

After a short tour of the city we set off for Ellora, thirty kilometres northwest, to see the cave temples and monasteries representing Buddhist, Hindu and Jain art cut in the rock in the final centuries of the first millennium AD.

The landscape, tranquil with little variation, kept us company on the journey. The weather was good, the time passed . . . and we began to adjust to the environment . . . when suddenly, without warning, as we rounded a bend, we beheld an unexpected sight. The rock of the hill had been cut away and in it had been hewn huge temples with statues, columns, sculptures and carvings.

Rock-cut temple at Ellora

Buddha in Ellora cave

The first thought was, why here? Why, in this ordinary landscape, had men thought to work so hard, to dig, to carve the stone in order to worship god through their creations? Whatever god, since each had made something for his own god.

I remember elsewhere, in other countries, the great works, the grand architectural monuments, were built in prominent places; they dominated the regions and ruled the landscape, their presence complementing the grandeur of nature, contributing to man's elevation. I remember too that the great works of art that set their seal on man's course on earth were made by the great, who employed the small, their workers, to make them. Here, the works we marvel at are the conscious effort of simple, small-great men who voluntarily dedicated their lives, cutting the rock, carving the stone, to offer their work to an anonymous god . . . . their god.

When the car stopped I remained immobile for a long time, gazing at the rock with its numerous man-made openings. As I gazed, I drifted out of this world, this noon hour, out of today, yesterday, the conventions of time. I let myself be transported back over the centuries to this very spot, the same spot where the first person had stood to look at the great porous monolith, and decided to cut, to carve, to create temples and monasteries, by himself . . . with what resources!

I felt myself disappearing, vanishing, in front of the power and majesty of that human being . . . who, knowing his nothingness, decided to embark on a struggle which far surpasses human limits man's abilities and says the great 'Yes' to the principle of creation.

And he managed it. Alone or with others, who one after the other

continued what they found . . . in order to pass on the clew to the one below . . . eventually to pass on to eternity the ultimate bounty of faith, of patience, of elevation of the human spirit . . . pass on to the sphere of the divine.

I've no idea how long I stood like that. But at some moment . . . I felt myself baptised in the spirit that they had begun and sown generously on the rock and in the surrounding areas. I let my steps guide me through the temples and monasteries, one by one. At the beginning were the Buddhist caves, then Hindu and finally Jain.

The scale of work required for each monument is unbelievable. You dig, you remove material in order to create what you have in mind, with what remains. There is no room for mistake . . . what you spoil cannot be corrected. A task which demands planning, prudence, patience and persistence . . . and above all, devotion to what you are doing.

The culmination of the work here is the enormous Kailasa temple, dedicated to Shiva, the god of life and of sin. The god of the senses and the god of man. Man, small and weak, who when aware of his failings and insignificance achieves great deeds.

The Kailasa Temple at Ellora

Entrance to an Ajanta Cave

It is a replica, you could say, of the god's legendary sojourn on Mount Kailasa in the Himalayas. The Kailasa temple at Ellora is the largest monolithic structure in the world, twice the area of the Parthenon and one-and-a-half times as high.

Outside the central sanctuary is a host of altars and shrines. All full of statues and reliefs, representations from the great Indian epics.

I walked about for hours, admiring, digesting, my being stretched taut . . . like a chord . . . all the time ... until daylight began to disappear. I had to return to the world of men and their mundane pursuits.

• • •

The next day we had an early morning start, for the road to the Ajanta hills was long and we had to get there early in order to be initiated into the other mystagogy of the human soul, the Ajanta caves.

The landscape through which we passed was soft and fertile . . . small cultivated fields . . . planted with cotton, sunflowers and cereals, tended by men with the same tools and in the same way as they had been for centuries. The plough drawn by the buffalo tilling the earth, the human hand weeding the field. Sheaves of wheat stacked without machines. But with the farmer who knows what he is doing, who feels the warmth of the soil, the sharpness of the thorn, the wetness of the mud, who feels too the joy of water trickling through his fingers, who loves to live with the senses heightened and the mind alert . . . the doors and windows open to the sun and wind, to the rain and snow. Every so often you pass by a village, a swarm of small dwellings, with a constant drone of voices, murmurs . . . and

Ajanta Painting

Ajanta caves

movements, of these slender people, full of vitality, though dry, gaunt, with just enough flesh to cover their bones and sinews . . . and colours. Colours everywhere, on the clothes, on the buffaloes, on the wagons, on the trees. Couldn't life be just colours or sounds?

The Ajanta caves do not take you by surprise. The road leads you there gradually. An overture, you could say, to the symphony you will shortly see and hear.

The car stopped at the bottom of a crescent-shaped valley. The cave-temples are hewn half-way up the precipice, formed in such a way that to see them you have to go up and down steps and walk along artificial corridors, which lead you to the beginning of the semicircle.

There you stop again. What was achieved at Ajanta began much earlier than at Ellora. Here the landscape attracts you, it compels you to stop and say: I shall build here, I shall create a temple so that I and those who will come after me can be transmuted into the divine, the unique, the One.

So, between the second century BC and the fifth century AD monks and masons toiled, with the most primitive of tools and systems of mirrors in order to illuminate their workplace, to remove thousands of tons of stone, and to paint the temples and monasteries we marvel at today.

The temples and monasteries are Buddhist. Here, in contrast to Ellora, the walls are painted with scenes from the life of the Enlightened One – the Buddha. Simple scenes, everyday scenes, human. The vivid colours have not been dimmed by the passage of centuries . . . and we can enjoy them today.

You walk and wonder, discover and delight . . . at the human effort, man's abilities, so harmoniously suited to nature.

How many times do you feel proud to have been born a man?

This feeling was uppermost in my mind as I followed the path back, far richer than when I had set out, more mature for the journey ahead in this country-continent.

Varanasi
The Sacred City

← *Varanasi: the west bank of the river Ganga*

On the flight to Varanasi, I called to mind books read years ago, images jumbled with the recent experiences of the past few days, here on the soil of India.

Varanasi (Benares, Kashi) lies on the west bank of the River Ganga, as it follows its crescentic course between Delhi and Calcutta. Once the capital of the ancient kingdom of Kashi, Varanasi has been the religious capital of the Indians ever since the dawn of history. To this day, it is the microcosm of Indian life.

The name Varanasi derives from the tributary of the Ganga, the Varana (Barna) which washes the northern and north-eastern flanks of the ancient city, and the river Asi. When Buddha lived in this region, shortly before the fifth century BC, there was already an ancient settlement on this site. Contemporary with Babylon, Nineveh and Egyptian Thebes, Varanasi is one of the world's most ancient cities, a mesh of deep-rooted traditions. It is the desire of every Hindu to visit Varanasi at least once in his life time, to be cleansed of his sins by bathing in the waters of the river Ganga. When

he gets old and dies within the sacred city, he is redeemed from the cycle of rebirths, which is the ultimate aim of the Hindus. This redemption means eternal union with the *Brahman*, 'the impeccable, inmovable serenity that never changes'.

The Ganga rises in the Himalayas and crosses the plain, debouching into the Bay of Bengal. Sanctified by the god Shiva, it flows slowly to the sea. Its holy waters transform Varanasi into a sublime purgatory. For this reason, Varanasi is dedicated to Shiva. Every year millions of pilgrims throng the narrow streets of this city of two thousand temples, altars and hermitages. A dip in the Ganga is an innate compulsion for the people here, born of the catalytic influence of their civilisation and religion. Characteristic of

A patchwork of clothes spread out to dry on the left bank of the Ganga

this is the wish of the first Indian Prime Minister, Jawaharlal Nehru, that after his death, his ashes be cast in the Ganga. He said:

> 'When I die, I should like my body to be cremated . . . A small handful of my ash should be thrown into the Ganga at Allahabad . . . has no religious significance, so far as I am concerned. I have been attached to the Ganga and Yamuna rivers in Allahabad ever since my childhood and, as I have grown older, this attachment has grown . . . . The Ganga especially is the river of India, beloved of her people, round which are intertwined . . . her hopes and fears, her songs of triumph, her victories and her defeats. She has been a symbol of India's age-long civilisation, ever-changing, ever-flowing, and yet ever the same Ganga . . .

Pilgrims bathing in the sanctified waters of the holy river

Ganga has been to me a symbol and a memory of the past of India, running into the present and flowing on to the great ocean of the future'.

These, my thoughts, heightened by a strong sense of anticipation, were interrupted by the jolt of the wheels on the landing strip of the airport.

And so I too came as a pilgrim to this holy city . . . expecting to see, hear and feel its effect on my 'Being'. As soon as we left the airport building and came outside, we felt oppressed by a stifling atmosphere, mingled with a heavy, indeterminate fragrance . . . something between incense, jasmine, sweat, fried oil, created by the herbs and whatever else was burning . . . at every corner of the city.

A young flower-seller

After witnessing a slight altercation between drivers, we arrived at a beautiful hotel, just like those you find in the English countryside – clean and comfortable. Soon after settling ourselves in its spacious rooms, we left to visit Sarnath.

Sarnath, a settlement, or rather an archaeological site now, a few kilometres north-east of Varanasi, is the spiritual centre of the Buddhist world, just as Varanasi is the spiritual centre for Hindus. Here, 2500 years ago, Gautama Siddhartha preached his first sermon, presenting the Eightfold Path which leads to the end of sorrow and to inner peace, enlightenment and, finally, *Nirvana*. Here Buddha established the doctrine of the Middle Way, the golden path which lies between extreme asceticism and the satisfaction of all desires.

Tibetan monks in their saffron habits have come to the Stupa to fulfil their vow

Two hundred years later, Ashoka, emperor of the Maurya dynasty and the greatest convert to Buddhism, came here. At Lumbini, the birthplace of Buddha, in Nepal (near its borders with India), Ashoka set up a column, and at Sarnath he built many *stupas* or pagodas. We visited the museum, a simple brown-stone building in a lovely well-kept park, which is rich in finds of that period . . . outstanding among them is the lion column capital, that faces you as you enter the museum. Dating from the time of Buddha, this capital symbolises the ideals of peace and virtue; it was later adopted as the national emblem of India.

Pilgrims place lighted candles on special stands beside the Dameh Stupa, creating a river of flickering flames

Below lie the ruins, with the remnants of glory that once symbolised this place where Buddhism, a religion in which the greater part of the population of the planet now believes, began.

A tranquil, verdant landscape is dominated by the great Dameh pagoda, built around AD 500 to mark the spot where Buddha set in motion the Wheel of the Law . . . . and all around are the ruins . . . . among creeping plants which embrace the stone, placing it in the here and now . . . giving the present picture of life that continues at its own pace. So that the words of the guide telling us what happened here seemed to be coming from far away.

Seated on a marble drum of an ancient column, we watched time while the speaker continued speaking, while the sun was setting . . . life which continues to dominate the ruins.

Monks from Tibet in their saffron robes ran round and round the *stupa* (had they vowed to complete a certain number of circles before returning home?) . . . happy that they had executed the divine command.

Sarnath, The huge Dameh Stupa

Next to the *stupa*, devotees lit small candles set on special stands, a row of flames flickering in the light breath of the air.

Further off, in a recently-built temple uniting the foundations of seven monasteries, the faithful chanted supplications and praised god, bringing the landscape to life. We learnt that on the anniversary of the founding of the temple – the first full moon each November – monks and laymen come here from all over Asia, to pray to their god. Before we left we bought carrots to feed the deer in the deerpark which is located here.

The next day we set off early – before daybreak – to visit the sacred river and to take part in a ritual repeated daily on the left bank of the Ganga.

We left the car some two hundred metres from the river and mixed in with the milling crowd, progressing amidst cows, flowers and odours which permeated our clothes and penetrated our skin. Heavy, heady odours reigned – preparing us for the mystagogy we were about to experience. The air dank, dense – you could cut it with a knife, as we advanced in the darkness, towards the steps of the *ghats*.

Bead shops

Paved landings and wide steps lead the believers to the river. Every *ghat* has its own purpose (for bathing, cremation etc.), history and tradition.

The murky river, churned up by the people pressing ahead to step into the sacred waters, filthy and slimy – which for the Indians assumes another meaning . . . from that which can be logically defined.

Boats, large and small, bob slowly up and down at the quay, full of colourful costumes . . . and lamps, little lamps, placed on leaves, float, tracing luminous patterns on the water . . . Gradually dimming even as the light tries to break in upon the darkness.

We boarded a sailing craft and moved away from the bank, to follow the river's flow and to see at close hand the ritual being celebrated along the left bank.

The buildings of the city began to appear, silhouetted in the slowly suffusing dawn light, giving the landscape a different aspect.

Behold, the half-ruined palaces of *maharajas*, mosques with minarets, Hindu temples with high pyramidal vaults, towers, hospices for the priests . . . a melodic medley of styles . . . Indian, Chinese, Persian, Mughal, even Italian Renaissance . . . an impressive and imposing set.

As the boat sailed on, borne mainly by the current and the indolent movements of the oarsman, we too began to feel as a part of the One.

There we felt, for the first time in many years . . . men's faith in something different . . . from what we in the West are used to.

We saw human faith in the godly expressed in singular and sundry

ways, depending on the pilgrim who has come from afar to be transubstantiated into the divine.

We saw men swimming in the sacred waters, washing, letting themselves drift with the current . . . others kneeling, solitary, meditating, transubstantiated at some point. Still others bringing the corpse of their loved ones, bedecked with flowers, to cremate it on the banks of the river on pyres of wood and perfumes, and to cast the ash into the waters that would lead the last remnants of their earthly presence to union with the Whole . . .

The ash and the water will enrich the earth that receives the seed which, in turn, will bear fruit, giving life to other creatures, who will follow the same wheel of life.

On the right bank of the river we saw the sun, transformed into a crimson disc – slowly rising – dispelling this mystery to which we were witnesses . . . and giving life its rhythm of daily functions. Dressing, walking, tasting fruits, singing, falling in love, shouting for joy . . . life that continues to rule in the world.

Small boats moored beside the ghats

We landed ashore, to follow a path through life. The city beside the river, a muddle of huts, houses and shops interrupted by narrow streets and alleyways, teeming with people. People of all ages and races – old men with biblical countenances, naked children, young women in colourful *saris*, old women with dishevelled hair and a distant look. And cows, the sacred animals, mixed with the crowd, ambling along slowly, watching . . . and a host of monkeys . . . everywhere.

Countless vendors, some sitting cross-legged, others running behind us crying out loud, pestering us to purchase something . . . a few flowers, a flute, a card, a doll . . . a god.

We began our tour of the city, pushing and shoving to make our way . . . we, a mass of the moving mass . . . that did not move on but stirred and swayed, on the same spot, like the ocean wave that swells and falls lapping the rocks . . .

And we discovered . . . here a temple, exquisitely beautiful, stuck in the mud, full of pilgrims . . . there a beggar, maimed, showing you his multilated limb

Ghat with prasad sellers

to get a rupee .... look a leper, a singer, a musician ... here a holy man, a *guru*, shut away in his hole, with a lamp lit at the edge .... for you to venerate and ask for his blessing. A petition for a favourable judgement that will finally release you from the eternal cycle of rebirth, and will unite you with the *Brahman,* the ultimate destination .... the One.

After wandering for what seemed hours, enchanted yet bewildered by all we saw – inside and outside our milieu ... we reached the temple of the bloodthirsty goddess Durga, the monkey temple. A quiet, run-down place with a few adorants in the temple and numerous monkeys outside, scampering unhindered, playing, unwittingly giving delightful performances ... that complete the contrasts of this city, this country, which have struck us since the moment we set foot in India.

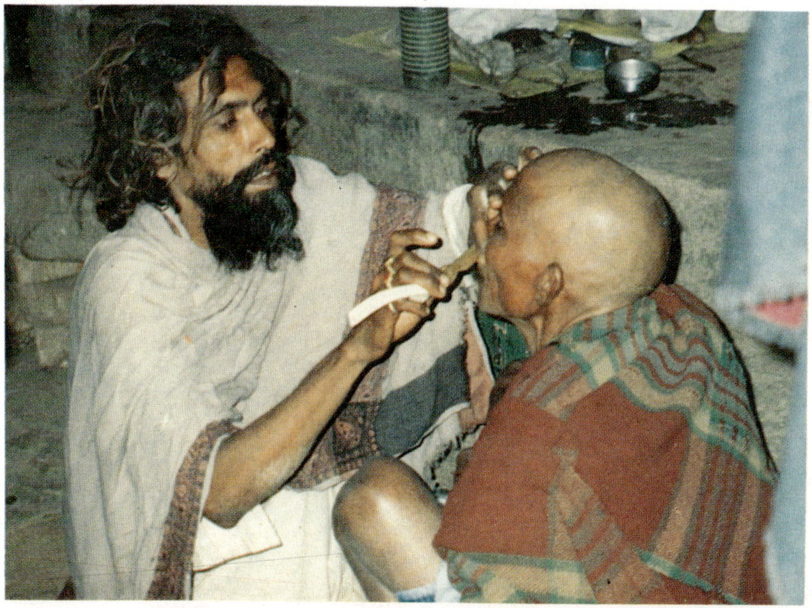

A barber shaves his customer at the kerbside

A Taste of Indian Religion

People from the West who visit India – influenced by their monotheistic religion – cannot understand the philosophy sovereign in this different world. The more you read about Hinduism, the faith of four-fifths of the population of India, the less you feel you know about it.

Over the centuries no one has emerged here to formulate rules or doctrines. As you delve deep into the countless texts, you are faced with a mass of confused possibilities and opposites.

Every now and then a new text emerges or a leader acquires devotees through his convincing teaching and virtuous life. But when the *guru* dies the personification of his teaching is lost too. Hinduism is like a sponge which absorbes whatever is good, right and exemplary. But what is exemplary is unique and not offered in imitations.

Indian temples, like those of the ancient Greeks, are not used for communal worship by the faithful. They are religious monuments dedicated to a god, in return for the bounties he bestows on men.

In India one can pray to whoever he wishes, wherever he wishes and whenever he wishes. There are no fixed dates and times, nor a locus for

← *A Sadhu, a holy man, absorbed in the scriptures*

religious ceremonies. Prayers can be said in a bedroom, in front of a private altar or shrine, in a farmstead, in front of a shrub or at the root of a tree, usually a fig (or banyan) tree – in many places, held as sacred by the Hindus.

Indians adore and enjoy festivals. Pilgrims flock to the temples and cities to celebrate anniversaries or religious rituals. At these no hymns are heard, but songs and music. The scene one gets to see varies depending upon the event, and is adapted to the legend identified with the god.

So on the anniversary of Krishna's birth concerts are organised and adorants sing . . . in honour of the god, who was an accomplished flute-player. In spring is the festival of *Holi* to honour the trees – called 'flames of the forest' – when their red leaves begin to open. On this day Indians forget their sorrows, sing and paint their face with coloured powders – green, red and yellow.

As a rule, Indians make no distinction between the sacred and the secular. Their whole life is full of holiness and they participate in the process of the universe as harmoniously as possible. Every act is also a rite. There is a ritual way to eat, to wash, to make love. The microcosm is connected harmoniously to the macrocosm and every action performed correctly, every rite, summons the cosmic forces that are called gods.

One could say that in India there are no gods – only symbols of various forms of energy or special-forces working in the world. But all of them have their source in the same, unique deity, like the colours of a prism that appear different yet are, in reality, no more than variations springing from the unique solar light. This deity cannot be named or ascribed to categories.

Ultimate reality begins at the point where thoughts, arts and sciences end, for which reason the ancient sages used opposite concepts to describe it: 'He is not this, nor that'.

Man comes close to god only when he can surpass himself. He achieves this transcendence through meditation which, though it begins from one point, must be intransitive. This is achieved through *yoga* – which helps in the suspension of all kinetic thought. Through meditation one can reach serenity and the void – about which we know nothing but which our efforts must tend to approach. This is the meaning of the *Upanishads*. The *Upanishads* which were written after the *Vedas* – the earliest texts in Indian literature – are inspired poems written by sages who gathered to exchange their religious beliefs and revelations, while imbibing the sacred drink, *soma*.

The *Upanishads* express a philosophy of the highest imagination ever born of the human mind. It would be no exaggeration to say that the *Upanishads* are the basic source of Indian thought and civilisation. These writings not only inspired the orthodox Indian philosophical systems but some others too, known as 'heterodox schools', such as that of Buddhism. Their spirit, either intact or reflected by Buddhism, influences the spiritual life of nations far beyond the Indian borders, such as Japan, Korea, Tibet, Ceylon, China and elsewhere. The *Upanishads* are not only of considerable historical interest with regard to the evolution of philosophy in India, but are indubitably of exceptional interest to the present era.

As time passed, Hinduism concentrated and combined revelations which allow each one, according to his wishes and potential, to find fulfilment by choosing his gods.

The diversity of texts and the plethora of peoples that created India gave to each god thousands of forms and names. Deeds and legends became myths which vitalised the substrate of the divine element. That is why these gods do not have their own life story. For each one there exist different explanations and variations referring to their birth, deeds and death. Every believer chooses whatever he likes, and every region has its own version of the events and the truth. India is full of long, lovely stories no one ever tires of hearing.

A bead seller spreads his wares in the street

Brahman is the name given to the balancing force that created the world. *Brahman* is the unique supreme being. Without beginning and without end, in space and in time, it has no form; it is the fount of all wisdom, joy, knowledge, truth. *Brahman* is not mentioned in the *Vedas*. It was born in the brain of Vishnu – as mentioned in the two great Indian epics, the *Mahabharata* and the *Ramayana*.

Brahman is the great architect, the supreme sovereign, the author of the *Vedas*. All is a dream, a symbol. It is India's view that nothing really exists. Every creation is full of void – indeed, just as today's physicists maintain – and this void is itself empty.

Every god has a symbolic animal – a vehicle. *Brahman* sits upon a goose, the symbol of knowledge. He has a consort, Sarasvati, goddess of speech and music. However, this goddess like all the others – since every god has his partner – is the personification of the god's energy. She does not exist either.

Vishnu is the name that was given to the axis of the world. He is the god who ensures the continuity of life and the smooth course of the cosmos. In order to achieve this, Vishnu dreams. Vishnu's vehicle is a bird – half-man, half-vulture – called Garuda. His consort is Lakshmi, goddess of wealth.

Shiva is the name that was given to the centrifugal force of decay. He is the god who destroys and creates, the god of time and of death. He is also known as 'the Pure One', 'the Great God' and 'the Lord of Light Sleep'. He is perhaps the oldest god in the Indian pantheon.

A scene of Jatayu- marana (from Ramayana)

Whatever has a beginning has also an end. Whatever exists will one day be destroyed. Whatever has grown and developed will be dissolved. From this dispersal, however, something new will be born. Since destruction is the prime cause of creation, Shiva remains both at the beginning and at the end.

Shiva has 1008 names and two aspects. One is that of 'the terrible', that destroys our life. The other is 'the good', that liberates us from a deceptive life and opens up for us the possibility of participating in eternal life.

Among Shiva's many wives, the most important are the very beautiful Parvati, the daughter of the mountain Uma, the serenity of the night Durga, the inapproachable Kali, the black one, the goddess of time, the terrible one, the great goddess, the personification of energy.

These three principal gods and others – there are said to be 333 million of them – have children and adventures. In long discussions at the temples and teashops, every believer has the opportunity to extol the qualities and powers of his favoured deity.

Some follow the teachings of Krishna – a form of Vishnu – who preaches that love is a means of liberation and devotion a means of salvation.

The deity is at the centre and man on the periphery. Every man follows his own path, according to his level of evolution and his abilities, in order to be rid of the cycle of birth and death as quickly as possible. Every Indian knows that sooner or later he will be united with the divine.

Christians, Jews, Muslims base eternal salvation on just one life .... they will either win or lose. The Hindu has eternity before him, which at some time he will gain. Life, they say, is a game for the entertainment of the gods. That is why Hinduism is perhaps not a religion, as we understand it, but a way of life, an art of living.

Khajuraho
The Dream

Khajuraho is a dream, a fairytale, written many years ago, that narrates the life of gods, kings and princes in a happy period of history. In a period when people and men elsewhere in the world were trying to find their paths and ways of expressing them, here in Khajuraho, south of the Ganga plain and north of the Deccan plateau, the land prospered under the rule of the Chandellas – a dynasty of Rajput, a Hindu class claiming descent from an original military, ruling caste. In its rich forests ran animals friendly to men, there was water in abundance, everything was an inspiration for the poets and artists of the age. Nature, in its generosity, provided wonderful materials in the quarries of the region, from which men built the temples and monuments of Khajuraho.

Myths and legends, ancient literature and inscriptions, present the history of Khajuraho as a riddle – for some elements are still missing to complete the picture. Some links have been lost in the chain of continuity.

A folk ballad of the seventeenth century relates a lovely legend concerning the origin of the Chandella dynasty.

Once, the legend goes, there was a young princess, Hemavati, whose heavenly beauty caught the attention of the moon god Chandra. One night, as Hemavati was bathing in the river, Chandra transformed himself into a handsome youth and seduced her. Of this union of a god and a mortal was born a son, blessed by the gods, courageous and fearless. One of his feats of valour was to kill a lion with his bare hands. This heroic figure is said to have founded the kingdom of the Chandellas. The emblem of the dynasty, appropriately, depicts a young man wrestling with a lion . . . and in Khajuraho there are many sculptures representing this scene.

The story of the moon god and the princess is surely imaginary, but it is not unusual. In northern India, in particular, princes were often said to have descended from the sun, Surya or the moon, Chandra and their power and status was deified.

With the creation of this legend, the Chandellas, who started out as chieftains, built up their foundations, gained strength and eventually became mighty rulers, who reigned here between the tenth and the eleventh century. Their capital was Khajuraho.

This was the age when India was the Eldorado of Asia. Men were wealthy, the soil was fertile, life was brimful of pleasures. The seclusion of women had not yet been established, to exclude them from earthly delights. Everyone lived a felicitous life in the tenth century, attending feasts and festivals, enjoying hunts, theatre, music and dance.

This unprecedented affluence cultivated the ideal clime for creativity, that culminated in the ultimate form of aesthetic expression, the building of

↑ *Lakshmana Temple*
Kandaria Mahadev Temple →

temples. There were no distinctions between the sacred and the profane. The temple was the house of the god, but it was also a hall for meetings, the locus of social intercourse and centre of gossip. The offerings of the faithful filled the purses of the Rajput ruler and he, in turn, gave to his people by supervising the construction of more temples – a happy, healthy circle that led to the creation of 85 temples in a hundred years. These temples were built at a time when architects and sculptors had passed beyond the classical and sophisticated stages to showy baroque, the dawn of the artistic power of the Chandella period.

We arrived at this dream at twilight, after the early morning mystagogy on the Ganga and our wanderings through the cobbled streets of Varanasi . . . full of thoughts and impressions.

Just as a storm is followed by the calm . . . so the greatest trial of the soul was destined to be followed by the celebration of life.

After we had settled into a beautiful, new hotel – that too, of the Chandella style, we had a bath and went to bed early, so as to be fresh for our tour of the temples of Khajuraho the next morning.

A splendid day dawned. The clear sun and the light air drew us outside to celebrate the glory of life. The small village we passed on the short road to the archaeological site was hardly a reminder of the important role this region had played in history. The dwellings, whitewashed huts with tiled roofs, are scattered right and left. Children play heedlessly at the roadside – with improvised toys – building their dreams below the bright blue sky. On entering the archaeological site you see the temples before you.

Constructed of yellowish stone tinged with brick red – except for a couple that are of granite – they stand on low platforms, their pointed vaults piercing the sky, in order to come closer to heaven, like a row of summits of the Himalayas, the mythical abode of the gods of the Indian pantheon.

The temples of Khajuraho represent the culmination of the Indo-Aryan style, as it evolved over the centuries. They belong to the north Indian Nagara category, but have certain special, distinctive features that make them unique in the entire land. Though they are dedicated to different deities, Shiva, Vishnu, or the Jain Tirthankaras – founders of a sacred order in the Jain faith – they display the same characteristics.

A Hindu temple is built to sanctify a holy place or to protect a revered object. An external staircase leads to the open portico of the entrance and then to the chamber in which the people once stood to observe the religious rites, that were accompanied by sacred dances, music and chants. Next to the chamber was the shrine in which the idol was kept.

In the larger temples, the central shrine was surrounded by a corridor, connected with other, smaller shrines – one in each corner – dedicated to lesser deities.

The temples of Khajuraho are remarkable for their quality and perfection, rather than for their size. Their architecture exhibits a harmony of proportions and a graceful plasticity. An unbelievably rich and impressive sculpted decoration is seen in the buildings. They are an example of the fruitful collaboration of two arts, architecture and sculpture, to produce masterpieces. Here, architecture is sculpture.

The temples are arranged in three groups, the western, the eastern and the southern, which are completed by tiny temples scattered here and there. No explanation for this can be given today – since the plan of the city as it was in those times is unknown.

We entered the archaeological site that encloses the western group of temples, and went through a wonderful, fairytale park, gazing at the temples, which came nearer and loomed larger at every step, slowly reducing our own presence to nothing. We sat down on a bench and, still from a distance, looked at the harmony created by nature hand-in-hand with man, centuries ago, and which still has something to offer visitors. Tall trees and bushes dotting a grassy carpet and small animals uninhibitedly moving to and fro convey a sense of tranquility and eternity. The sense of eternal existence before and after us – definitive for the continuity of the cosmos.

You could stay for hours, days, years on the same spot, just looking – escaping time which rules us with artificial, human problems – to be transmuted, You, into the divine, consubstantial One.

We got up, I don't know after how long, and followed the guide in order to join the others and see the temples at close hand.

The Lakshmana temple, dedicated to Vishnu, one of the earliest of the western group, has five shrines – a central one for Vishnu and four ancillary

↖ *Couple locked in embrace*

Side page:
Loving couple, horses and an amorous female
←

ones at the edges. It is a perfect example of a five-shrined temple. The lintel over the entrance to the central shrine shows Lakshmi, goddess of wealth and consort of Vishnu, together with Brahma and Shiva. A host of reliefs embellish the temple's interior and exterior, illustrating struggles of gods, humans and animals from the legends of the Indian pantheon.

Still trying to overcome the sense of beauty, you walk a few paces and . . . behold, more temples.

Opposite stand the Vishvanatha and Nandi temples, which share the same platform, with two stair-landings, one flanked by two lions and the other by two elephants. One is dedicated to Shiva and the other to his sacred bull, Nandi.

A little beyond is a small, seemingly insignificant temple, originally dedicated to Vishnu, but who was later replaced by the river goddess Ganga who sits on the back of a crocodile. Our guide referred to it as the shrine of Parvati, Shiva's wife. As always, truth and lie are jests of time.

As you walk, you are exhilarated by what man made, what nature creates in the world. You walk and you see, you see and you are satiated . . . and there, in front of you, . . . the temple of Kandariya Mahadev, the most mangificent at Khajuraho, built on a long, elevated terrace which it shares with the Devi Jagadambi temple. The three-metre platform on which the temple stands and its pyramidal vault soaring 30.5 metres into the sky, allude to Shiva's sojourn in the cave on Mount Kailasa in the Himalayas. Encircling the pinnacle of the temple, small, identical pyramidal structures rise skywards and complete the work – a work unique in the world.

Lord Ganesha

Details of pillars

A host of statues in zones cover the outside and the inside of the temple. In a wonderful game of light and shadow, an endless parade of gods, men and animals, a stupendous row of nude female bodies, clad only in jewellery. They are goddesses, dancing girls and heavenly nymphs. All radiate grace, charm and youth. Each one in a different pose, a different movement, a different occupation. Every part of their body, every detail

Jain temples

– breasts, legs, shoulders – every curve lovingly and artfully carved. The cold stone takes on all the warmth and pulse of living flesh. Their faces express tenderness, pride, joy, emotion, desire, sorrow, expectancy, pleasure, ecstasy.

Among the goddesses, the dancing girls and the chaste nymphs, appear – defying all modesty – bold, realistic fugures, superb compositions full of vitality. There are erotic couples of gods and men, and scandalous groups of more than two persons. An endless variety of extravagant erotic poses, of unbridled sensuousness, indescribable provocativeness, caressing, kissing, embracing and making love.

The West has focused on these erotic scences and picked them out as the principal element of the art of Khajuraho, presenting them and condemning them as pornographic exhibitionism revealing moral baseness and lack of purity.

The truth is that all these sculptures are works that demanded hours and hours of patience and persistence from (to us, anonymous) craftsmen who laboured to embellish the resplendent edifices we admire today.

We continued wandering among the temples, on the soft grass, in the absolute calm of the landscape, and reached the eastern group, a few kilometres farther off.

The eastern group is located close to the village and comprises six temples – three Hindu, dedicated to Brahma, Baman (Vishnu in a dwarf incarnation) and Jabari (Vishnu), and three Jain that are still in use. So as we entered the fenced site we saw a crowd of people milling around sanctimoniously in order to pray to otheir own gods.

Jainism, a breakaway sect of Hinduism, was created in the sixth century BC by Mahavir who, like the Buddha, was a hermit preaching a simple, moderate way of life. Many rich merchants were converted to the new religion, which advocated social equality unlike Hinduism which divides men into castes and places merchants lower in the hierarchy than brahmins, and kshatriyas – the caste of warriors, politicians and administrators. Even today, wealthy communities of merchants belong to this religion-sect and build temples and shrines.

We mingled with the crowd and let our steps follow those of the devotees. The temples here lack the architectural grandeur of those of the western group – they are far more human, I would say – but they have lavish and intricate decoration, the culmination being the Parshwanath temple – the largest of the group – which is adorned with wonderful sculpted representations, everyone of them a work of art. You can stand transfixed for hours and hours, admiring the statues. Beauties with gorgeous eyes, children, flowers and all manner of ornaments, in astonishing compositions. A statue of Shiva and Parvati is the epitome of amorous love, the god's hand caressing his lover's breast . . . and their eyes, captivated by each other's beauty, gaze full of tenderness and desire.

We left, full of this beauty, to return to the hotel. But we could not shake off a crowd of little children who pulled us and pestered us to buy something – a souvenir – from the small folk art shops that are found outside every archaeological site. So we walked by each of the little tin shops, chock-a-block with various bronzes, pottery, silver jewellery, statues and whatever else you can imagine.

I wanted to buy a small bronze statue of Shiva to remind me – when I return to Greece – of the other approach to life that has today, in this problem-filled world, special significance and value.

The guide led us to what looked, from the outside, like a humble little house but which, on entering, surprises you with its size and the countless

objects arranged in categories, according to the type, with tremendous care and skill.

The room full of carpets, the room full of little wooden statues. Over there, jewellery – of silver and semi-precious stones – placed in cases, attracts your attention . . . in front, the *saris*, hundreds of lengths of material with which Indian women swathe their bodies, using them as dresses. Colours . . . bold colours. The Indians, like nature, are not afraid of colour contrasts, ... and they are right. The result is astonishing.

We wandered round and we looked, we looked and we admired, handling the small bronze objects zealously made by craftsmen.

In India the old has no intrinsic worth – as in the West – because craftsmen are still working in the same way as their ancestors worked, two and three hundred years ago.

A bronze statuette of Shiva, and a little painted wooden elephant accompained us as we left the shop, along with a silver postal cylinder, used in the old days for correspondence, and a bronze necklace, the purchase of my friends accompanying me on the journey.

And pleased with the cultural feast we had enjoyed on that beautiful, brilliant day, we returned to the hotel to collect our things and leave for the airport.

Agra

The City of the Mughals

It was already dark when the aeroplane took off. Wedged between two Indians busy emptying the contents of the small tray brought by the air hostess, I drifted into my own private world. Full of the experiences of the day, I was preparing myself for the new world the morrow would bring.

Agra, the city identified with the great Mughal emperor Akbar, who made it fair and famous. Little is known of its early history. Babur, the conqueror, descendant of Timur and grandfather of Akbar, founded the first important centre here. How strange it is that the descendants of the war-loving Mongols (Persian *Mughal,* properly a Mongol) – who set out from what is today southern Russia – should develop into the most refined rulers of their time. The Mughals adored art, were eager to learn, and displayed a tolerance that is rare in history. The golden age of Agra ended in the seventeenth century, after its climax, in the reign of Shah Jahan, who built the Taj Mahal.

Nothing significant happened in Agra before the Mughals, and nothing after them. Plundered and destroyed by the Marathas, the city fell

EPSI

into a peaceful lethargy in 1803, when it was captured by the British. Today Agra is the highspot of India for every traveller, who comes to see its supreme creations, the Agra Fort and the Taj Mahal.

These were my thoughts as we landed at Agra airport and were driven to a wonderful hotel, to rest and get ready to see those creations that the mature and sensitive Mughal leaders have bequeathed to mankind.

We set off in the morning to visit the Taj Mahal, one of the world's most renowned monuments. Only a handful of travellers who visit India do not come to Agra to admire the Taj Mahal. For some it is on par with the Parthenon and Egypt's Pyramids, among the aesthetic masterpieces of civilisation. For others, it is simply the tangible testimony of one of the world's greatest love stories. For me, however, these classifications, regardless of literary presentations and architectural achievements, are a matter of personal taste.

Moreover, before visiting this monument, I considered it essential to learn something of its history. In contrast to other edifices, built either as an expression of religious piety or out of the vanity of princes and kings, the Taj Mahal is a memento of love.

At the age of twenty-one, Anjuman Banu Begum (Mumtaz Mahal), niece of the queen of Jehangir, Noor Jahan, married the Emperor Shah Jahan, grandson of Akbar. Many are the tales that are told . . . of her generosity and wisdom . . . both as mistress of the palace and as adviser to her royal husband. However, all these are overshadowed by the love that she had for Shah Jahan. She bore him fourteen children, and died delivering the fourteenth child in 1630, at Burhanpur on the Deccan

Previous pages:
(Left) *The Agra Fort*
(Right) *The Taj Mahal*

plateau, where her husband was campaigning.

Her death struck Shah Jahan like a thunderbolt. His hair turned white in a few months and he discarded his splendid raiment . . . for sombre costumes. Six months after Mumtaz's death, her body, which had been buried temporarily at Burhanpur, was brought to Agra in a splendid procession. Shah Jahan vowed to build a monument that would outshine in beauty and luxury whatever existed in the world. And to this end he brought artificers from all corners of earth – Persians, Frenchmen, Italians and a host of others. He assembled a huge army of twenty thousand craftsmen and workmen who built a new village – Taj Ganj, which exists to this day – in which they lived. Construction of the Taj Mahal commenced in 1632 and it took seventeen years to complete.

We reached the entrance to the monument which, unlike other Mughal mausoleums, is not a single structure but a complex of buildings. The space outside was crammed with cows, and vendors tried to sell us some trinkets. We passed through the gateway and into the courtyard of the outer complex. The arched and vaulted red-brick buildings introduce the visitor to his imminent initiation. Large trees complement the man-made creations, leading you to the entrance gate. Tall and towering, it too is of red brick, elegantly built and decorated with excerpts from the *Qur'an*.

Usually, the buildings supplementary to the central monument are notable architectural structures. Not so here. Here, everything is contrived to emphasise the central monument, and the visitor passes by the other buildings without really noticing them. On coming out of the gateway, you find yourself directly facing the monument, and stand immobile, transfixed

Intricate reliefs in the Red Fort

and enchanted by the harmony imposed by its symmetry and line.

The Taj Mahal is a gigantic building, set near the river, on a wide terrace paved with marble. It is surrounded by vast gardens with beautifully designed, blossom-filled flowerbeds, canals, water jets, fountains and rows of cypress trees. Made entirely of snow-white marble, with delicately wrought relief decorations, it is mirrored in the oblong lake in front of it. At the corners of the terrace stand four tall, elegant minarets with triple balconies, like lighthouses that guide sailors safely to harbour.

Entrance gate of Sikandra

To the right and left of the monument rise two other red buildings. The left is a mosque with three vaults, the Javab or Echo mosque. But since the orientation of this building is not correct for its use as a mosque, it is thought that it was intended for accommodating visitors to the tomb. However, its *raison d'être* is obvious: it maintains the architectural equilibrium of the monument and the symmetry of the structure.

We walked slowly across the garden spread out before the monument, captivated by its symmetry and harmony, amidst a multitude of pilgrims and visitors, who too had come to pay due respect to their faith in human creation, or in the love written and expressed in this way – centuries ago – that shows the depth of human devotion to your fellow man, your helpmate in life, who shares your feelings of joy, pain and pleasure.

Then we followed the others, the many. We took off our shoes, went up the steps that lead to the platform and entered the central chamber. There, in the half-light, are two tombs – that of Mumtaz Mahal at the centre, and the tomb of Shah Jahan. Their marble is studded with precious and semi-precious stones: emeralds, rubies, diamonds, turquoise, topaz, coral, onyx, lapis lazuli. The walls are inscribed with passages from the *Qur'an* and inlaid with polychrome flowers, formed with pieces of coloured marble, embedded in the white marble with unparalleled and unbelievable technical perfection.

Before leaving, we walked round and round several times, in order to take in and take with us the image of what is, without doubt, a unique work. A work that made us ponder over the questions that crowd the mind . . . what is right, what should be done . . . what counts . . . in this life?

On emerging from the courtyard of the outer complex, we mixed again with the moving-static crowd, through which we passed with difficulty to reach the car. We were driven a short distance along the narrow, shop-lined streets, jostled by bicycles, carts, animals and people, to another great human creation, the fort of Agra.

Here in the fort of Agra, that slice of history of the Mughal Empire, from Akbar to his son Jehangir and his grandson Shah Jahan, is imprinted with stones. The rust red of the walls erected by Akbar and the gleaming white marble of the palaces built by Shah Jahan. An impressive ensemble built on the banks of the Yamuna river – that runs through Delhi, descends to Agra, and finally flows into the Ganga, the holy river.

We arrived at the Amar Singh, the south entrance of the Agra Fort, since the west side of the fort is not open to visitors as it houses military installations. We looked up at the red outer walls, which loomed above us – twenty-one metres high – covering our field of vision. A simple construction, not lavish at all, which filled with trepidation any invader who thought of besieging the fort. The walls were two-and-a-half kilometres in length.

We crossed the drawbridge that leads to the gate and were led through a maze of corridors at right angles. This daedalic approach was designed to confuse and avert would-be attackers, making it impossible for them to use any kind of siege-machine. We approached a moat, twelve metres wide, and then another wall, the inner, that rises up sheer. The inside of the gate astonished us with the beauty of its architecture. A comparatively small, central arch was surrounded by solid supports covered by domes,

and linked with corridors connecting the various battle stands. All these were decorated with blue tiles, emphasising the Islamic influence on the austere Mughal architecture of the fort.

After standing for quite some time, gazing awestruck at the red stone all around us – wondering how the enemy would have felt – we went up the steep ramp leading, between the vertical walls, to the palaces. These walls constitute an additional defensive measure against assailants who, even if they managed to pass through the gate, would, as they went up the ramp leading to the palaces, be an easy target for the fort's defenders, who could aim at them from atop the ramparts. Furthermore, it is said that this steep ramp and the arrangement of space hindered the flight of the attackers, who could not easily escape.

Having let our minds enter the atmosphere of that age with these thoughts, we reached the esplanade. Facing us was a large, square building of white marble, an enormous low structure with nine arches at the edges and slim columns supporting the roof.

This building, the *Dewan-e-Aam*, was used for public audiences and large receptions. In a huge hall with finely-worked marble columns upholding intricately-carved, denticulate arches, was a throne embellished with precious stones, one of the masterpieces

← *Stone-carving, a craft with a long tradition*

Itmad-ud-Daulah →

of Mughal art. Below the throne was the seat of the grand vizier, the prime minister. To the right and left of it were the places for seating the nobles and dignitaries. Here, the Europeans and other emissaries came to pay their respects to the emperor. Here, the emperor dispensed justice to his subjects, rich and poor.

On both sides of the large courtyard in front of the building, under gold-embroidered awnings, the commonfolk stood, with arms crossed. Each, in turn had to bow three times before approaching the grand vizier, and did not dare lift his eyes to look at the emperor. The herald announced the name of the person standing before the Emperor, the 'Sun of the World'. A French traveller who saw the Great Mughal recounts: 'The monarch, everyday at noon, sat on the throne with some of his sons seated to the right and left of him, while eunuchs stood behind him and wafted away the flies with peacock plumes, stirring the air with large fans which they moved rhythmically, humbly waiting to carry out any service asked of them'.

Today, centuries later, we, like all the visitors, were able to wander in the halls of the palace which then – apart from the public audience chamber – were not for the use of all.

First we visited the *Jehangir Mahal*, the unique palace built by Akbar in 1570. Here Akbar's ability to add elements of native architecture to the style brought from central Asia, can be clearly seen. Columns, corridors, courtyards, two-storey façades – the remnants of decoration conjure up a feeling of the majesty that existed in those days of glory. We went through the rooms one by one, and were astonished by the complexity of the composition and yet the functionality of this building.

Many palaces some independent, others adjoining, were later built next to the *Jehangir Mahal* which is the largest building in the fort of Agra. Among them was the *Khas Mahal* (private palace) built by Shah Jahan in 1637 . . . a white marble building with flowers incised on the walls of its bathing area, with archways inlaid with precious and semi-precious stones, and terraces with a view of the Yamuna river.

There we stood looking down on the river . . . a shallow stream, wending its serpentine way . . . across the plain. Over there, on the same bank, the Taj Mahal dominates by virtue of its harmonious presence. In front of us the vertical walls of the fort gave us the feeling of power in the region, of power which was paramount for many years over this land – a foreign land for the first Mughal. Power which was not just based on military force but also on the political maturity and wisdom of the Mughal rulers.

We continued admiring the halls of the palace, which cover an enormous area . . . the palace of the mirrors, the garden of vines, the women's apartments . . . until we finally descended the ramp that leads to the entrance gate.

From the white marble to the red stone . . . two strong colours that come from the depths of the earth of India . . . which in the hands of the right men are matched and used to advantage . . . so that they leave behind them the trace of their creative passage.

A short respite at our hotel refreshed and renewed us. Straight after lunch we prepared for our journey by car to the other fort-palace, in the enigmatic city of Fatehpur Sikri.

Fatehpur Sikri

The City of Victory

During the early years of his reign, Akbar was worried because none of his wives was able to give him a son, an heir. The sons who were born died in infancy. Akbar consulted a wise 'holy man', the Muslim saint Salim Chishti who lived as a hermit at Sikri, in the hills forty miles west of Agra. When Salim Chishti was informed of the emperor's worries, he foretold the birth of three boys. Not long afterwards, one of Akbar's pregnant wives — a Rajput princess of Amber — was brought to Sikri with her attendant so that the auspicious prophecy could be fulfilled.

On 30th August 1569, Akbar's wife was delivered of a son, who was named Salim — after the holy man. He was Akbar's successor, the future Emperor Jehangir. In March the following year, another of Akbar's wives who stayed at Sikri, gave birth to another son.

Akbar's initial reaction to these happy events was to make a pilgrimage on foot to the Muslim holy man. Two years later, however, he proceeded further . . . and, as a token of his respect for Salim Chishti, began building an enormous mosque and an imperial palace on the hills of Sikri. The nobles of his court followed suit, building fine houses all around. Ramparts were constructed to protect the area. So a city was born. And after Akbar's victory in Gujarat in 1572-73, 'Fatehpur' was appended to Sikri (for 'City of Victory').

It was raining while we were travelling to Fatehpur Sikri . . . a fine drizzle to water the plants . . . the sky was grey and the clouds low. The plain we crossed was lushly verdant, with pronounced variations of colour, interrupted here and there by the yellow of mustard flowers and the dark tones of the freshly ploughed soil. The cows – here, fat – grazed in the fields, seemingly free and content compared with those that wander along the tarmac streets of the city. There were a few houses, here and there, indicating man's presence.

The contrast between the city and the countryside is catalytic. As you leave behind the seething crowd, you feel you are suddenly entering another world, where the serenity of the landscape relaxes you and prepares you for the next surprise.

And there, in the middle of the road, was a gypsy dragging two ambling bears by their chains. I recalled Sikelianos's poem about the Sacred Way, that leads to Eleusis, and I asked the guide to stop . . . He refused politely: 'If we stop', he said 'the gypsy will pull at the chains for the bears to dance . . . to earn a little money . . . but the chain hurts the animal, and it's a shame'. A simple argument that taught us a lesson and made manifest the sensitivity of this ordinary man who – expressing the sensitivity of a people – follows another way of life, different from that which we are used to. A sensitivity that dominates the whole country.

Elaborately carved pillar in the Dewan-e-Khas

Panch Mahal

Man lives – and should live – in conciliation with all creatures that follow the same course on earth . . . to be born, to grow up, to die. And we are all bound to take this same course . . . in comradeship, harmony and love.

We continued on our way, passing by the cultivated fields along the road that was, in the heyday of Fatehpur Sikri, one long, continuous market-place. A contemporary British merchant, describing this route, wrote that when journeying in the countryside between the two cities (Agra and

Fatehpur Sikri) you felt you were in an inhabited region all the way.

Fatehpur Sikri is built on the top of a line of rocky hills. The difficulty of the location chosen by the Mughal emperor was no problem to him. He simply ordered that the hilltop be cut away, in order to build a city. With a nod of the head he created an artificial lake in the foothills of the range – thirty-three kilometers long. This lake protects one side of the city, while the other three sides are protected by solid ramparts. Here, as in the fort at Agra, impressive buildings were erected, with splendid audience chambers, reception halls and private apartments with stepped roofs.

The architectural unity of Fatehpur Sikri is truly admirable. It is the work of renowned architects, specialised gardeners, marble carvers and all manner of craftsmen, whose collective endeavour created this wonderful complex. A remarkable water supply system had even been prepared, though this was never fully operative because of insufficient water. This along with successive misfortunes were the reasons why this opulent city of dreams was abandoned.

We drove through one of the external gates, left the car at the entrance to the palace and walked across the courtyards to enter it. It was still raining. What strikes one instantly on seeing the palace is its colour . . . dark red . . . on the roof titles, the stones, the floor slabs . . . everywhere. Here there is one colour. The falling rain gave it an even darker, lustrous shade, against the backdrop of the sombre sky.

Salim Chisti Dargah

The palace at Fatehpur Sikri comprises a sequence of contiguous rectangular courtyards, aligned on axes, that create the various groups of buildings. As in most of the palaces of this period, it is divided into three main parts, the women's quarters, the men's quarters and the areas open to the public.

We wandered through the rooms and courtyards, went up onto the terraces and examined the columns, the carvings, the corridors. All executed with consummate care and skill, an aesthetic delight for the visitor.

Every building is different, to serve its particular function. Every stone correctly placed, to constitute an element of the whole, just as every man's obligation in the world is to constitute a small, infinitesimal element of the Whole.

Night was beginning to fall when we got back into the car to return to Agra. The route seemed colourless and monotonous in the dark. The blinding lights of the oncoming cars, the sudden swerves to avoid a cyclist, a pedestrian, an animal wandering aimlessly along with a false sense of security. It was late when we reached the hotel. Time for dinner.

Indians are abstemious. Having sanctified the large animals, the bovines – cows, buffaloes, calves – a choice was made thousands of years ago, to prevent the disappearance of these animals, that not their meat but their products, milk, cheese, yoghurt and butter be used for human sustenance.

These as a basis, together with what the earth produces – flour, rice, pulses and all kinds of vegetables – offer a varied menu enhanced by the addition of an amazing range of spices. The Indians are basically vegetarian and their diet frugal. They use their bread – a staple element of their meal – made of maize flour baked on a slab in the oven or fried in a pan with a little sunflower oil, to wrap a morsel of rice or lentils, which is accompanied by boiled vegetables, chicken or fish. In order to reduce the heat of the spices, which dominate all flavours, a little yoghurt is taken to cool the mouth.

Hungry after our tour, which satiated us with spiritual food – reserves for use when we return to Greece and look back on the experiences acquired on this journey, and ponder over our path in life – we shared out the flat bread and ate the rice, lentils and yoghurt. Then we went to sleep, in order to rise early next morning for the journey to Delhi, and thence to Rajasthan, the state of the *maharajas*, the warriors who stemmed the incursions of invaders who, at various times, tried to conquer the fertile plains of India, seeking richer lands in which to live.

← *A simple hut in the countryside*

On the Roads

The distance between Agra and Delhi is two hundred kilometres. This trip, from the earliest seat of the Mughal empire to the present capital of modern India, offers a protracted peregrination in history as well as the ethereal beauty of history.

We set off early in the morning. The dull, rainy weather made it difficult for the driver to go more quickly along the royal road, laid by the Mughal emperors in the sixteenth and seventeenth centuries, when the capital was moved from Agra to Delhi. Today the 'royal road' looks like a provincial metalled road in a European country. When it rains it becomes slippery and a death-trap, for the lorries, loaded haphazardly with all manner of merchandise and men, lose their balance all too easily and topple over on the kerbside. This situation is exacerbated by the worn-out tyres and brakes, whose level of resistance is low.

We drove along slowly and carefully to avoid unforeseen dangers, which appeared all the time. Sometimes . . . a car from the opposite lane, skimming past us at a hair's breadth. Sometimes . . . a cart that drew up without warning for the driver to fix the parcels he was carrying. Sometimes

. . . a cyclist speeding along in the middle of the road. A little beyond we had to stop because a truck had skidded and blocked the road. All the passengers travelling in it, pushing and heaving, managed to pull it to the edge . . . to open the road again. And so we continued our eventful journey.

However, what attracts our attention, as foreigners, seems quite natural here, since these are problems everyone lives with and faces in his own way, absolutely unflustered, unhurried . . . since time here has no meaning – it runs independently of men's life, which sometimes becomes infuriatingly cheap with indifference to basic natural rules.

It is India's attempt to adjust to the new *status quo* of the technological revolution . . . which is faced with a phlegmatic indifference . . . where every single thing is termed natural . . . and when an accident happens . . . it simply happens.

The landscape we were crossing was much the same as that we had seen on our route from Agra to Fatehpur Sikri, with the difference that here there were clear signs that we were approaching the capital. Small houses right and left, and here and there a factory or a board indicating the site of a future factory or warehouse. The nearer we got to Delhi, the greater was the density of buildings on its outskirts.

It took as long for us to reach our hotel in Delhi as it had taken to reach the outskirts of the city. Once there we had a break and a rest, because we were leaving that very evening, by train, for a one-week tour of the state of Rajasthan.

When we planned this journey we decided to see Rajasthan by taking

a special train, the 'Palace on Wheels'.

The 'Palace on Wheels' is rather like a cruise ship in concept. You travel for a week, staying on the train – which basically travels at night and arrives at a city in the morning, giving you the opportunity to sight-see all day and return to the train in the evening . . . to go to the next city.

The advantage to us of this choice was that by leaving our luggage on the train, we were relieved of the task of transporting it . . . and furthermore, in this way we could see far more places than we would in the same period of time using an aeroplane or the regular train.

We arrived at the train in the evening and settled in our carriage. After our meal in the restaurant car, the train set off slowly . . . for our first destination . . . Jaipur, capital of Rajasthan.

Rajasthan
The Land of Valour and Honour

I was awakened at daybreak by the steady swaying of the train as it ran along, clicking upon the tracks, creating an echoing rattle . . . which only our fatigued minds and weary bodies could silence.

As I looked out of the window I saw the silhouettes of passing trees, human figures intent on their daily tasks . . . herds of cows or flocks of sheep grazing. The weather began to improve. The clouds dispersed, leaving the blue sky free for the sun to shine forth from the firmament, casting shadows here and there.

Now and again, a house, surrounded by children, it seemed like thousands of children, in colourful clothes, their clever, sparkling eyes gazing at you, trying to give you . . . love.

I remembered the dedication in an Indian book I had flicked through recently . . . 'To my mother who taught me to love and to give'.

I tried to recall all I had read – many years ago – about Rajasthan and the men who lived and who live in this Indian state. 'The Rajput know how to fight a battle, but they do not know how to win it,' the Mughal emperor Babur had said.

Rajasthan is the land of valour and honour the land where the women proceed to the funeral pyres of their husbands, to be burnt with them, so as to fufil their ultimate duty. In this land of chivalry and courtesy it was natural to dine with your adversary after an engagement in the arena of war, since the warrior castes inexplicably claim ancestry from the sun and the moon.

This land, where the earth is scorched by the sun and where the rains are rare, is coloured by people who defy the monotony of the grey-brown sand with the splendour of their garments and jewellery.

Rajasthan, rich in history, legends and traditions, was originally divided into twenty-two principalities, each ruled by a prince, the Rajput.

Since olden days conflicts for the control of northern India, between the Hindu Rajputs – who were, and still are, accomplished horsemen – and the mighty Muslims have been legendary, both on the field of battle and in all manner of subterfuge.

A tale is told of an eleventh-century Hindu leader who led an army of Muslim invaders into the desert . . . where they lost their way and died of thirst.

Aware of the martial abilities of the Rajputs and wishing to rule the country without continual wars, the Mughal emperor Akbar adopted a unifying strategy, different from the dogma of divide and rule. In order to expand his empire to Rajasthan, he married a Rajput princess from Jaipur.

In coiled turban and sitting cross-legged, the man enjoys his hookah →

Dancing in typical Rajasthani dresses

She, as we have learnt already, was the mother of Jehangir. Many of Akbar's trusted generals were Rajputs too, who had formerly fought against him. Indeed Akbar appointed a Rajput, Man Singh, as governor of a large province in the Mughal empire.

The chivalry of the Rajasthan princes brings to mind that of the feudal lords and the knights of the West, and the Samurai of Japan . . . for whom honour and glory were part and parcel of their daily life . . . life that gives rise to legends that become examples from which the fabric of human behaviour is woven.

Kathputlies

Though these independent princes were obliged to become part of the single state of India after Independence, they kept – and still keep – the ownership of their palaces, their large estates, their jewels and enjoyed many other privileges. They refused to forsake, under any circumstances, their princely way of life. Moreover, as recompense for their loss of political control in the region, the Indian government granted them a stipend which was regularly paid until 1973. Then it was concelled along with the other privileges by Prime Minister Indira Gandhi, who felt the princes had received enough from the poor Indian state.

Even so, Rajasthan preserves the character of the country of the Rajput legends, with its palaces, its strongholds and, above all, its all-pervasive dreamy atmosphere that veils every building, every story, transforming every element into a link in a fairytale – one that we were to soon experience.

This reverie on the past was rudely interrupted by the shudder of the wheels as we came to a halt at the railway station in Jaipur.

Jaipur
The Rose-Hued City

Waiting for us, as we came out of the railway station, were two elephants, bedecked in brightly-coloured cloths and garlands, upon which sat Indians in turbans and traditional costumes. Beside them, men, women and little children, all in local costumes, welcomed us, presenting us with garlands of flowers. In the background were the sustained strains of the distinctive music you here all the time in India. It was a glorious day. The bright blue sky and the shining sun heightened the colours, shortened the shadows and created an atmosphere of joy and optimism. So, gaily and full of expectations, we got into the cars and headed for the city.

Jaipur, the rose-hued city that rises shimmering from the yellow-black landscape of the Aravalli hills, has been the capital of Rajasthan for two hundred and fifty years. Its history began in AD 951 and is spun with legends and tales that unravel like a ball of yarn, full of wars, intrigue and romance. Its name derives from Maharaja Jai Singh II ('Jaipur' means 'City of Jai'), who became king of Amber in 1699, at the age of thirteen.

At that time the strength of the Mughal empire had weakened and

City Palace

Ganesh Pole

there was no reason for the Rajputs to hide in strongholds and forts tucked away in the mountains. They could now come down to the fertile plains, without fear. So, shortly after his accession to the throne, Jai Singh decided the time had come for him to transfer the capital from the rock-girt fort of Amber to the adjacent plain. Jai Singh swelled his court with architects, artists, astronomers and many intellectuals, and in 1727 drew up plans for his new capital. Its refined, roseate buildings are described in historical accounts as the 'shade of an autumn sunset'.

We reached the city and continued our way through the jostling throng

Jantar Mantar

Suhag Mandir

on foot. Dust, laden camels, horses, dogs, people and countless bicycles made a vivid picture, but nothing conjured up memories of a gilded, frontier city in its heyday. However, if you look beyond the scene of God's moving creatures, you get the sense that Jaipur is a city with a wonderful layout, wide streets, designed to be a capital. Most of the houses and buildings, of all kinds, are built of pinkish stone and make a pronounced and pleasant impression on the visitor.

We walked and looked, and felt the rhythm of life in the old city manifest in all things, animate and inanimate. As we drew near to the bazaar, teeming with people, our attention was focused on the crowd that got thicker and thicker . . . until suddenly we saw before us an imposing, five-storey, rose-coloured building . . . the *Hawa Mahal* . . . 'the palace of winds' . . . which stands strange and aloof from all that life has created around it.

The strange, ornate edifice, built in rose-hued stone, takes its name from the westerly winds which send a refreshing breeze through its casements, cooling the rooms and other interior areas. Its façade resembles the cells of a honeycomb. The semi-octagonal projecting windows with perforated tracery screens – from where the ladies of the court could watch what was going on in the streets – transport us into another world, another age . . . especially when the setting sun sets the butts and bays of the palace aflame, as the light falls on the corners and recesses of its faces. The roof is curved with vaults and finials, harmoniously completing the architectural structure.

We stood for some time admiring the work . . . the work of men who laboured for hours, days and years to achieve their goal. Anonymous yet happy, as all men are who reach their journey's end . . . their Ithaca.

Time had passed more quickly than we realised. Obeying the call of the tourist guide, who had told us we must leave in order to have time to visit Amber . . . we tore ourselves away. We passed through one of the seven wonderful gates of Jaipur and found ourselves in the countryside, on the way to Amber.

For six centuries Amber was the capital of Rajasthan and the nucleus of the history of the Rajputs. Today, it is no more than a ruined city, with a

The five-storey rose-coloured palace of winds, the Hawa Mahal
↓

The Central Museum

ruined palace, surrounded by magnificent fortifications, built on the top of a hill. Construction of the palace was begun in 1700 by Man Singh, and it lasted one hundred years. It shows a synthesis of Mughal and Rajput architecture.

We crossed the green landscape and were aware of the change in scenery that gradually prepared us on the mental plane . . . for the impressive sight we were about to see.

On our right we passed the huge artificial lake with the *Jal Mahal* palace in the middle, a royal lodge once used by the princes when out hunting ducks. Today the lake is dirty, the stagnant water murky and slimy green, and the *Jal Mahal* dilapidated and crumbling.

The road became steeper and steeper as we made our way up through small valleys and ravines, full of trees and bushes, until, at a turn, another picture came into view . . . a palace set on high, built on the summit and the sides of a precipitous crag. A beautifully designed building that inspires respect and repels any would-be assailant.

As we drew near, the palace took on other dimensions and was transformed, giving the symphony another tone. When you enter the valley of the flowers and pass through the rose-hued gate, the palace of Amber lights up with shades of colour and nobility.

To reach the palace you have to go up a steep road that passes through a succession of gateways leading to the central courtyard.

We chose to cover this route on the back of an elephant, which, like its companions, was adorned with multicoloured garlands, straps and flowers. These, together with the necklace of tiny tinkling bells around its neck, made our journey even pleasanter as we swayed from the rhythmical rocking of the animal's ponderous gait.

The courtyard, a spacious esplanade, offered an overall view of the complex building. Staircases, ramps, stepped roofs enclose the functional areas of the palace.

We wandered here and there . . . The main hall, known as the hall of victory, with its alabaster coffering, its beautiful mosaics in pale, pastel shades and its various handicrafts for which Jaipur is famous. The rooms small, almost intimate, as if for the family – a Mughal influence. The sequence of courtyards and the narrow corridors are typical features of Rajput architecture. The traces of former glory are apparent everywhere ... especially in the *Sheesh Mahal*, the hall of mirrors. It is now an established custom for visitors to enter, close the doors and light a match, and then look up at the ceiling, brilliant and glowing with the reflections of the flame on the gems and marble.

Before leaving the palace, we went up through the corridors and chambers to the terraces ... to see the spectacular view from the site on which it was built.

Opposite, on a higher hill, stands the fort of Nahargarh. There they guarded the royal treasures, and on that peak the *maharaja* went into retreat, to relax and to revel in the vista of the sunset and the view spread out from the palace.

Jal-Mahal

On the way back, as we descended the steps of the palace to reach the gate, we halted, ecstatic and intrigued by the spectacle of dozens of monkeys playing, scampering, leaping and caressing. A spectacle more charming than any perfectly directed performance, enacted on the fences, the walls and the roofs . . . spontaneously. An expression of joy for the lovely day, the few peanuts . . . and nothing else. An expression of the joy of life, that asks no more than those simple pleasures only life can offer, and which we have almost forgotten.

We stopped for lunch at an old palace that had been converted into a very handsome hotel, with all comforts. Set in the midst of a well-kept park, it had tennis courts, an indoor swimming pool and all other facilities one could wish for in a first-class hotel.

After a wonderful meal we lounged in the comfortable armchairs on the veranda, enjoying the lovely view and the fine weather. You often come across such special delights in India . . . where indigence exists side by side with luxury, luxury one cannot easily come by in European cities.

When we had rested from our morning excursion, which had drawn up the curtain on the world of the Rajputs, we visited the palace in the city.

We passed through the east gate, the central one, and went into a complex of buildings, a maze of kiosks, courtyards, halls and palatial mansions, constructed over a period of time by the *maharajas* ruling the region.

The first building we saw on entering was the *Mubarak Mahal* kiosk-guest house. Built of marble and stone, it is decorated with ornate marble tracery and encloses the old guest house. It now houses a costume and textile museum, with all manner of attire – from royal raiment to simple silk garments – a symphony in colour such as you frequently come across in this land.

We came down into the courtyard again, to visit each one of the buildings ranged round it . . . the war museum and the art museum, which houses a collection of miniatures of the Mughals and various Rajput schools, rare manuscripts and enormous carpets of 1600, originally laid on the floors of the Amber palace.

We walked and saw and admired what human hand had wrought. Over there the palace of the moon, the *Chandra Mahal,* beyond, in the centre of the inner courtyard, a pair of huge silver urns. In the private audience chamber, on a raised dais, wonderful marble columns.

It really needs a separate chapter for one to describe the many works of art, large and small, that abound in this building complex. Our time was limited . . . our schedule tight . . . and the purpose of our journey was to get a taste of this country . . . otherwise you need a great deal of time to tour India . . . months if not years . . . stopping at a different place everyday, if you want to get to know . . . the religion, the history, the art and the people of this land.

Time was passing and the day was nearly over. We went back to the train to continue our journey to the next stop. It was after nightfall when we realised, from the jolt of the wheels, . . . that Jaipur was now but a memory . . . seen for a short while . . . a vision that had entered our mind and lodged itself there for ever.

Chittorgarh
The Cradle of Courage

Our next stop was Chittorgarh, cradle of courage of the Rajputs. A city baptised in heroism, a source of inspiration and a point of reference. At one time capital of the principality of Mewar, it is now famous only for its castle. The castle of Chittor is linked in tradition with the seventh century and remained the capital until 1567, enjoying triumphs and suffering defeats. A bastion, the bastion of victory, is a reminder of the Rajput triumph over the Muslim kings of the neighbouring states.

Chittor was sacked three times.

The first in 1303, when a Muslim king tried to abduct the Rani Padmini, a very beautiful woman, said to be the loveliest in the world. The women of Chittor rivalled their menfolk in courage. When the battle turned in favour of the Muslims, the Rajput ladies lit an enormous pyre, donned their bridal robes and fell, singing, one after the other, into the flames. So when the last warrior fell fighting 'for the ashes of his parents and the temples of his gods', all that the conqueror found in the castle was the smoke from the fire, drifting up to heaven.

↑ *Details of Vijay Stambh*

← *Vijay Stambh*

The second was in 1535, by the sultan of Gujarat. Once again the Rajput, threatened with defeat, accepted death. The queen, having secured the escape of her young son, led the women to the pyre. Thousands of women burnt themselves, while thousands of warriors were slain on the field of battle.

The third attack took place in 1567, under Akbar, the great Mughal. The two leaders directing the defence in the fortress, Jaimal and Patta, so impressed Akbar that he had statues made of them in their honour – representing them seated on the back of two elephants – which he set up at the entrance to his palace at Agra.

It was past daybreak when we were awakened to get dressed and hop into the cars, in order to visit the castle of Chittor. The weather was dull and overcast. A morning mist covered the plain . . . so it was that we slowly began to discern what was evidently a mountain, pointed and steep, on top of which we could make out the structures of a gigantic castle. As we approached and the atmosphere cleared, we began to get an idea of the size of the fortress we were shortly to visit.

Samideshwar Temple

The castle is built on a sheer precipice formed by the mountain ridge, and covers an immense area. Its walls, high and well-built, are eleven kilometres long and dominate the whole of the surrounding region. Chittor, which rises 150 metres above the plain, fills you with awe even today, and is a splendid example of Indian defensive architecture.

We drove through the successive gates leading to the interior of the castle, then left the car and began to wander. We examined the buildings one by one . . . those still standing . . . and those in ruins, witnesses to the conflicts of the past.

A monument dedicated to the two young heroes killed here, attracts our attention . . . and further down, a loverly little Hindu temple, dedicated to Vishnu . . . and another, over there, dedicated to Krishna. Both temples are built at the edge of the fort, and from them we admired the view . . . of the plain below . . . which was becoming clearer . . . since the sun had begun to rise in the sky . . . and shed its dazzling light. Now we could distinguish the little houses of the town, the trees and the fields, which stretched as far as the eye could see.

We descended a little way in order to see a pool in which the *maharanis* used to bathe . . . with benches and couches at the edges. As we were climbing back up to the main level of the fort, we were confronted by the triumphal arch, a nine-storey, circular structure – thirty-five meters high –

Jain Kirti Stambh

with relief representations carved on its exterior. We wandered around Padmini's palace for a while, to the background of explanations and narrations by the guide, who reeled off incidents and details of events that time had transformed into legends . . . that intertwine with others, to create the folk ballads . . . spiritual food at festivals.

On our return we stopped at a Jain temple of the twelfth century, plain and beautiful . . . its many domes rising heavenwards, and came to the half-ruined palace, the *Rana Kumbha*, an outstanding example of the Indian royal complex. Stables, corridors, courtyards, halls, multi-storey constructions, balconies and terraces are the characteristic features of the palace.

We climbed up, clambered over and jumped here and there, to inspect every new element we saw. And we were the only visitors to this palace . . . once filled with music and the tinkling echo of the women's silver anklets.

As we were leaving to return to the train, I thought of the deserted ruins, which apart from their memories have no other companions but the monkeys and the vultures which hover and swoop . . . to take their fill, to the sound of the baying of the wolves heard now and then in the night.

We got into the car and took the road back, arriving quickly at the train . . . to continue our journey . . . for we were already late and still had a long day ahead of us.

A temple

Udaipur
The White City

It was not far to our next stop, Udaipur. The route was pretty, with small cultivated fields, trees and houses. All the way our eyes were glued to the window, so that we could take in as much as possible, to take back, as memories, to Greece . . . where, in our own home, we would unfold, one by one, the images and impressions acquired on this great journey.

Udaipur, capital of Mewar state, is called the 'city of dreams', and its nobles, the *maharanas*, are known as 'the sun of the Hindus', the highest rank in the Rajput hierarchy of the 'solar system'.

Udaipur was named after the *maharaja* Udai Singh, who founded the city in the mid-sixteenth century, when he escaped from Chittor after the third Muslim attack. Although his escape was not consistent with Rajput codes of honour and valour – which demanded struggle unto death – this city with its majestic palaces, in which we all delight today, vindicates his act.

← *A view of the rooftops of Udaipur*

According to another legend, Udai Singh was wandering in the plain, when he met a holy man who told him that if he built the city at the edge

City Palace

of the lake it would never be besieged. Udai Singh took this advice and built Udaipur. And Udaipur – in contrast to Jaipur, which is known as the rose-hued city – is called 'the white city', because of the sugar-white colour of its palaces.

We arrived when the sun was near its zenith . . . and were led to the Palace of the Lake, the Jaganiwas Palace, which has been converted into a luxury hotel.

It was not far, so we went along the narrow streets with the usual hordes of people, bicycles, carts. Then the picture changed completely. We

Mayur Mahal

continued our way across courtyards and atria, that constitute the entrance to the palaces and houses of the aristocrats . . . when suddenly, opposite to us, was a large lake, surrounded by steep shores and buildings.

And right in the middle, the palace . . . like an ocean liner . . . seeming to sail upon the grey-green waters, its reflection colouring the lake. The view from the quay on which we stood, awaiting the little boat to take us to the palace, was fantastic.

Behind us was a row of white, multi-storey façades of the city palace, rising up vertically at the water's edge. In front of us lay Lake Pichola – a man-made creation of the fourteenth-century imagination – with the palace in the middle. Close to it, on another islet-ship, another royal kiosk, the Jagmandir. Opposite, on the peak of one of the verdant hills surrounding the lake, stood another prominent palace.

As the environment began to take hold of us, we were transported to another age . . . to another world . . . far away from the everyday . . . to the land of dreams. We boarded the boat and a few minutes later disembarked at the palace.

This white marble building is a superb architectural achievement, for it combines beauty with functionality and puts you in a happy mood. A complex of apartments, courtyards, atria, fountains and gardens . . . that relieve the volumes and make life more human, giving the visitor variety and alternatives, to make his stay more comfortable and idyllic.

We wandered from room to room, from atrium to courtyard and corridor . . . mingling with the guests staying there. We peeped into a large suite – formerly the room of the *maharana* – an apartment designed with exquisite taste, with an enormous window and a little balcony directly above the lake . . . and a unique view . . . since it is also orientated so as to afford a sight of the very beautiful, majestic palaces on the opposite shore.

We freshened up and went to the restaurant for lunch. The quality of food and service was unrivalled. Nowhere else in the world, I would say, do you find anything comparable. And afterwards, as we strolled through the rooms of the palace-hotel, I thought to myself . . . how lovely it would be to be able to stay here . . . some time . . . for a week . . . away from the world, in company with the beauty so generously offered by nature, human imagination and skill, to all of us . . . who enjoy it centuries later.

We got into the boat again to cross the short distance separating us from land. As we were speeding along, I remembered a story . . . that relates that this creation was the result of a prince's obstinacy. When one day, so the story goes, Prince Jang Singh asked permission of his father, Amar Singh, to use the kiosk of Jagmandir – which is built on the other island – so that he and his friends could enjoy themselves, his father refused, saying he must build his own kiosk in which to enjoy himself. The prince, angered by his father's refusal, built the palace on the adjacent island . . . the one we had just left, and which is said to be one of the most romantic holiday hotels in the world today.

As we neared the shore, the *maharana*'s city palace . . . loomed larger and loftier, its high vertical walls rising sheer out of the water and its solid

Maharana Pratap Smarak →

octagonal towers roofed by vaults. This impressive construction is the largest palace in Rajasthan. And the antithesis between the two cities, Chittorgarh and Udaipur, is manifest: Chittorgarh – we had seen in the morning – is martial, masculine . . . while Udaipur is the city of peace, feminine . . . and it is India, the country that unites these two opposites, playing with love and life . . . wealth and poverty . . . beauty and ugliness . . . giving the traveller the opportunity to see and enjoy what he wants, to the extent his personality can absorb.

As we passed through the gate of the palace, a hostess asked us if we would like to meet the *maharana* of Udaipur, who resided in the opposite palace, his permanent home. We accepted with pleasure. We thought, it would be interesting to meet the descendant of those people who had once fought and ruled in the state of Rajasthan . . . and who still maintain enormous properties – even though their political privileges were abolished by Indira Gandhi in 1973. So we agreed to visit the *maharana*, after our tour of the city palace.

We went into a large courtyard, the entrance to the palace, surrounded on three sides by two-storey buildings once used by the guard and the *maharana*'s staff.

Dominating the other side is the white mass of the palace, nowadays set up as a museum and visited by foreigners and natives. The outside wall towers up to the sky – reminding us of the ramparts of Chittor. A medley of arches, vaults, turrets and battlements marks the roof of the palace-fort.

← *Lake Palace*

We wandered for hours in the royal apartments, noting the copious use of marble, coloured crystal, mirrors; the lavish carvings, the silver doors, the well-kept gardens and the fountains, which denote the discreet influence of the Mughals.

From the early years of the seventeenth century, a friendship had developed with the Mughals, kindled when *maharana* Karan Singh granted asylum to the son of the emperor Jehangir, who later ascended the throne. Displayed in the museum are the turbans the Mughals exchanged with the local princes in a gesture of amicability and goodwill.

Time passed and our hostess reminded us of the meeting that had been arranged with the *maharana*. So we hastened down the stairs, along the corridors and across the courtyards, into the courtyard of the modern palace, that stood opposite to us.

After the necessary checks, we were conducted to a reception hall to await the *maharana*'s arrival. The room, cluttered with furniture and objects. The walls covered with portraits and pictures, with no apparent rhyme or reason . . . except that they had to be there.

Before we had time to find our bearings and sit down on a seat . . . the *maharana* appeared – a man of medium stature, bald, with moustache and beard, dressed in an all-white costume – and greeted us in impeccable English.

We sat down and exchanged a few pleasantries, rather formal I would say. I felt this man was out of his element – living most of the time in America and Europe . . . and the only reason for his presence here was to keep an eye on the colossal fortune he had inherited from his audacious warrior ancestors for whom death held no terrors . . . when honour demanded it.

We bid the *maharana* goodbye . . . trying to recapture the dream that had enveloped us.

A respite, at sunset, was our visit to the *maharaja*'s garden, with its many large, dense trees, bushes, blossoming flowers in beds and fountains. A beautiful, peaceful ensemble. We walked under the shady arbour and came to an artificial lake, its shores dotted with marble statues of elephants, large and small, in various poses. Fountains and jets of water played onto the statues and the surface of the lake, creating a thick layer of droplets, suspended, dancing up and down, transporting us to a fantasy world far away from the mundane. To a world rid of all petty perspectives and ambitions.

Twilight came and the garden was closed to the public. We had to leave . . . tired from the day's activities, full of impressions. We happily began returning to the train. But as we were walking towards the car, the guide told us . . . that we really must visit a new village . . . built by the state . . . it would be a shame to miss it on our way back from Udaipur.

We were in a quandary, but not wishing to offend the guide, we agreed and got into the car. Night had already fallen on the city and the countryside. We drove along narrow roads, through twists and turns, and after quite some time came to a deserted spot.

We got out of the car and a short way off saw a really lovely little village . . . with its huts, museum, theatre, workshops . . . and a host of young people, men, women and children, each one acting his own role in the play called life. Here acrobats gave entertaining performances, there a swarm of children in colourful garments were dancing . . . to the accompaniment of instruments, vying with one another as to who would jump the highest, who would perform the best. Their faces smiling and their eyes gleaming in the darkness, which was pierced by the spotlights. Farther down in the workshops, women were weaving on their looms, craftsmen were chiselling silver and copper to make bracelets and other pieces of jewellery . . . that abound in this country. Over there, a museum, where the villagers proudly exhibited their handicrafts.

We walked about, charmed by the feast held here every day to celebrate the joy of life. We spoke with the people, and though not understanding their language made ourselves understood, with that disposition to communicate, to transmit to each other the messages concealed within us.

The way back seemed very quick – for our mood had changed completely – and the fatigue we had felt before gave way to delight. Man's mood can alter his physical responses and transform him.

We slept deep and undisturbed – a lion's sleep – without the swaying we had become used to . . . since the train stayed overnight in the station.

We spent the next morning in the city. Walking aimlessly in the narrow streets. It was a lovely day. The streets of Udaipur seemed less crowded in comparison with those of Jaipur and the other cities we had visited so far.

These carefree mornings are essential intervals in every journey. They give you the chance to let the impressions you have gathered soak in, to order your thoughts and to prepare you for the new things that are to come.

The ladies in our company were fascinated by the Indian textiles, woven on the loom in the traditional way. The colours and patterns are bold and beautiful, something we noticed from the very first moment we set foot in India . . . the women dress in amazing combinations of colours you never see in the West.

We watched the merchants spread out their wares and advertise them, and . . . the people crowding into the narrow aisles made by the piles of clothes displayed on the shelves . . . on the floor . . . in every corner that could possibly be used.

Jaisalmer
The Desert City

After this quiet morning, the time came for us to say goodbye to Udaipur and to board the train . . . for the longest leg of our journey . . . to cover the distance separating the white city of Udaipur from the desert city of Jaisalmer.

We travelled by day and so had the opportunity to enjoy the landscape we were crossing. We followed the same route as far as Chittor, the fort we had visited the previous morning on the way to Udaipur. The train then veered northwards and began to chug its way up the Aravalli hills. The terrain became more and more desolate and steep. Fewer trees, fewer fields . . . the faces of the people we passed were harsher . . . fewer flocks. Bends and bridges alternated as we approached the highest point.

The Aravalli hills, as they are called, is a mountain range from an old era of orogenesis. Over one thousand metres in altitude, they begin not far from Delhi and extend for five hundred kilometres in a northeast-southwest direction. The formation of the peaks and gorges is weird, reminiscent of modern paintings, as they take on strong, sombre colours, further intensified in the twilight as the sun goes down.

← *Bird-view of Jaisalmer city*

Night fell, and we, with our faces pressed to the window, tried to enjoy to the utmost the kaleidoscope of images all around . . . until the shapes became shadows . . . and everything was shrouded by the darkness . . . that covered the landscape. All we felt was the regular clickety-click of the wheels on the tracks, as the engine struggled to make its way up the slope.

As the movement of the train became smoother we realised we had passed through the hills and were now speeding across the plain. We slept soundly, in order to be all ready for the next day.

When we awoke in the morning the landscape had changed . . . we were travelling across the Thar desert. To our right and left was sand, with the occasional brush and cactus. Our introduction to a new experience.

The sun rose, further enhancing the desert landscape through which we were journeying. Like a ship crossing the ocean, that sees nothing but sea as far as the horizon, we saw nothing but sand and scrub, as far as the eye could see.

Jaisalmer is the westernmost city in India, lying close to the border with Pakistan. A tiny diamond in the heart of the great Thar desert, it was once the capital of the Rajput Bhati. A medieval city, set on low hills in the midst of a sea of sand, it is girt by stone walls five kilometres in length. It resembles a lofty vision in pale yellow, interrupted here and there by lush green oases.

The first impression of Jaisalmer is, I would say, of an ethereal place, marred somewhat when one delves a little into its past. Jaisalmer developed originally as an important caravan centre. Together with Bikaner and Jodhpur, set at the edge of the desert, they constituted the golden cities, the major centres on the ancient silk road linking Central Asia and Northern India with the harbours of Gujarat.

Long trains of camels carried gold and silver, silks and spices, cotton and pepper, sandalwood and camphor, ivory and opium, women and slaves, merchandise for sale. The nobles of Jaisalmer filled their coffers with money, levying taxes on those in transit . . . who not only paid these dues but were often robbed by the fierce and fearless dwellers in the desert.

These desert people, passionate men and exotic women, lived a harsh life, won every day and every night with struggles . . . struggles that became

Jaisalmer Durg

legends. This was the land of the Bhati caste and the Rathor of the Rajput.

Jaisalmer is like a dream come true, the fulfilment of a wondrous prophecy.

The myth of the Bhati – biblical in analogies – refers to forgotten nomadic peoples returning to the promised land. Their stories, described in the epic of the *Mahabharata*, were handed down from generation to generation, together with tales of their wanderings in inhospitable parts. Pursued and harassed, they ended up here, building a mighty fortress on a site picked by the Bhati chieftain, Jaisal, who later acceded to the throne.

Gadisar Lake

Rang Mahal,
Jaisalmer Durg

So, in AD 1156, the foundations of the fort were laid at Jaisalmer, atop the hill of Trikuta.

The train stopped at Jaisalmer station, which is quite some distance from the fort, the impressive mass of golden yellow sandstone that dominates all.

We passed through the series of gateways to the fort and the double ramparts, to reach the central square. All along one side of it stands the seven-storey palace, built between 1763 and 1820. A complex of buildings crowned by an enormous metal umbrella, which is affixed to a stone pole.

We took a closer look at the historic point, in front of the entrance to the palace, where the ladies of the court committed *sati*, immolating themselves on the funeral pyre after their husbands had been slain by the enemy who captured the fort in 1294.

Inside the fort are numerous Jain and Hindu temples, and many lovely mansions – the *havelis*.

We wandered through the alleyways running through this small settlement, stopping every now and then to look at a courtyard, a casement . . . a bridge connecting two houses over the street and, above all, the façades, appearing embroidered with carvings ... as if they were of lace. The result of much tiring work, demanding devotion, patience and persistence.

As we moved towards the edge of the internal settlement, we climbed up onto the bastion, from where we saw the city outside, spread out on the level area. Small houses, all the same, were scattered around the castle, built of the same stone and mud, throbbing with life. Men and animals bustling hither and thither all day long, like ants.

On our return from the bastion we passed by a complex of Jain temples, built on a knoll in the settlement. Their domes pierced the sky and their façades and interiors were crowded with thousands of statues of gods and dancers – groups from mythological representations.

Movement is the distinctive trait of these sculptures and statues. Movement that seems to have been frozen, instantly, when the artist finished his work. In one wing of the temple complex is the library, with a vast collection of old manuscripts – some of the twelfth century – written on palm leaves in black ink and bound in painted wooden covers.

Enchanted by the beauty we saw all around us, we came down slowly . . . and out of the fort into the city. We walked in the narrow streets, between the pale yellow, filigree houses we had seen just minutes ago from above. We pressed on, looking to right and left, until we came to a quarter with five large, wealthy mansions or *havelis*. These residences were built in 1800 by the Patva brothers and constitute the pinnacle of aesthetic refinement and beauty.

Light and airy structures with ornate architecture that endeavours to cater to every need in the desert. The buildings clamber upwards, to grasp the cool evening breeze, the balconies project in such a way that they protect the inside walls from the fierce sunlight. The perforated windows with their screens serve two purposes . . . they beautify the building and . . . shelter the women from prying eyes. Every opening, window or door, is

← *NathmalJi Ki Haveli*

Details of a haveli →

adorned with a fine, light decoration of flowers and geometric motifs.

We greedily devoured all we saw as we walked about in this quarter, surrounded by swarms of children, playing and dancing at every opening in the street. The children, with their vitality and intelligence, are one of the loveliest elements of this country. Quite apart from the pleasure they give to all who see them, they are a stable base, a hope for India's future development.

It was past midday when we left the neighbourhood of the *havelis*. We passed along the dusty street, through the noisy market-place with a multitude of people in front and behind, selling and bartering their wares. Peasants with furrowed faces leading tired horses, dragging carts, and haughty camels loaded with the produce from the village . . . . A scene that could well be out of the Middle Ages.

We ended up at a hotel restaurant for lunch. As we entered the courtyard we saw something the like of which we had never seen before . . . nor could we ever imagine. Two women, dressed in colourful *saris*, tall and slender . . . were plastering a wall with their bare hands . . . without any tool. They took the mud in their palms from a basin they were holding and slapped it to the wall . . . rubbing it to spread it, and to give it the desired texture. A task that anywhere else in the world would be done by workmen in work clothes using some kind of a trowel.

Women plastering a wall without any tool

We watched the simple, harmonious movements of the women, in their strong, mixed-up colours, who, intent on their task, were working noiselessly . . . simply, humanly.

The food at the restaurant was lentils and yoghurt . . . which we ate with a lusty appetite, sitting in a large room the uneven floor of which – of a mixture of clay and sand – was covered with handmade rugs.

That afternoon, we took an excursion into the desert. The calm heart of the desert lies at Sam, forty-five kilometres from Jaisalmer. Here in the stilliness of the night, watching the sand dunes being chased by the dry desert winds and transformed into fluid outlines, one can feel divine moments when the bright trajectory of a shooting star reveals man, eternity, the significant and the trivial in each of us.

After an hour-long journey through an arid expanse of sand, scrub and cactus, their leaves bearing tiny, modest mauve flowers, we reached Sam, one of the national parks of the desert. We were welcomed by a kiosk-guest house built on an eminence. A building, or rather a cluster of small cylindrical buildings of stone, in hues varying from brown to yellow, depending on the light and the time of day. We walked onto a belvedere formed in front of the buildings. The view was amazing.

Before us, like a sea, spread the desert, wavy with sand dunes as far as the eye could see. In the area formed lower down, hundreds of camels with their drivers, clad in colourful costumes, awaited the 'fare'. The 'fare' is a trip into the desert on the back of a camel.

We saw camels with tourists on their back and the drivers in front, pulling the rein . . . mounting the sandhills . . . to be lost in them . . . as ships

are engulfed in the tempestuous sea . . . sometimes bobbing on the waves . . . and sometimes disappearing into them.

We stood immobile for quite some time, rooted to the spot, observing all this mystagogy of nature . . . as the sun was slowly sinking . . . until the guide told us that it was time we had a camel ride.

The camels, sitting in the sand, patiently awaited their passengers. At a nod of the driver's head they rose, first on the hind legs . . . making you feel you are going to fall off if you do not clutch the saddle hard . . . then with a sudden shake, the creatures stood up completely.

The camel driver in front gives the signal for the trip to begin . . . The slow, rocking motion is strange at first . . . until you get used to it and adjust your body to the animal's gait . . . And then you gradually begin to enjoy the ride on the fine, grey-brown sand . . . Up and down we went. Seeing yet isolated from the environment, as the camel progressed in the desert.

Nothing helps you to pick your way . . . apart from the rules that are obtained at sea . . . the instinct innate in the animals . . . and acquired by their drivers, from long years of close contact with them.

We continued on, and the buildings of the kiosk

– when we saw them – became smaller. We rode on and on, deeper and deeper into the desert. We stopped for a break, dismounted the camels and decided to return to our starting point on foot.

Walking in the desert sand was an unprecedented experience for us. Our legs sunk in the fine sand. We felt that all around us was in a state of flux. We saw the dunes formed by the wind, in gentle ripples – as on the sea – and in denser folds when the wind became stronger. What, I wondered, is a sandstorm like in the desert . . . when the wild wind whips up whatever is in its path . . . blowing the sand into the sky and covering everything.

We climbed up the sand hills to get our bearings – by looking at the kiosk . . . and continued on in the same imaginary direction, when we walked down slopes and gulleys created by the sand.

When we reached the starting point the sun was touching the horizon. Darkness began to fall on the desert sand. The camel drivers mounted their beasts to return to their villages, which are at some distance from the national park. A journey into the night, without road, without guide . . . the only compass being the instinct of the camel and its driver, which is capable of leading the pair safely to the warmth of the stable and the house, worn out by the fatigue of the day and ready to enjoy the evening meal.

Our return to Jaisalmer in the night was uneventful. We were driven to the train for a short rest, and to prepare for the last sight Jaisalmer was to offer, late at night.

← *Pillars of a Jain temple*

Night-time in the desert is cold. The warmth the earth has absorbed from the sun's rays during the day is radiated back into the firmament. So there are extremes of temperature in the desert – hot by day and freezing cold at night.

Since the night's performance was scheduled to take place outside – in the courtyard of a hotel – bonfires had been lit to lessen the chill, to warm our feet and make our stay pleasant.

We sat as close to the fire as possible, wearing our warmest clothes . . . and, while eating, enjoyed the dancing girls swirling on the stage . . . dancing to the accompaniment of folk instruments, sensuous dances, religious dances, dances of life and lamentations of death.

Dance in India is a form of magic. The dancer is endowed with supernatural powers. His personality is transformed. As in the mental and physical discipline of *yoga* union with the Supreme Being is achieved, so in dance ecstasy is achieved through initiation into the divine. The dancer discovers the mystical essènce and is finally united with the divine essence.

Dance in India flowered alongside the strictness of initiation – fasting, breathing exercises and introspection. In order to enchant others, one must first enchant oneself. And this is achieved through prayer and dance. In this effort a prominent role is played by the god Shiva, the cosmic dancer, the lord of the dance. Shiva is the dancer of the universe. In his dance events, the eternal energy is at once concentrated and presented. The forces gathered together and made manifest in his madness, in a perpetual swirl, are the powers of the evolution, conservation and dissolution of the world. Nature and all creatures are the outcome of the eternal dance.

Shiva as dancer (Nataraja) is depicted in a series of exquisite bronze statues in southern India, of the tenth and eleventh centuries. The details

Children dancing

on these figures are explained allegorically by Hindus. In his raised right hand Shiva holds a drum, to keep the rhythm. This sound is the vehicle of speech, the bearer of the revelation, the tradition, the magical song and the divine truth. Further, the sound in India is identified with the ether, the first of the five elements of the divine essence. In his left hand, Shiva holds a tongue of fire. Fire is the element of the destruction of the world.

The serious mien of the dancing girls is characteristic. Dressed in colourful *saris*, their arms covered with bracelets, and jewels of all kinds covering the exposed parts of the face and body . . . they began moving harmoniously all the parts of their body – head, hands, feet, eyelids and

neck . . . and to mime scenes from everyday life, religious ceremonies, emotions of sorrow and joy . . . and amorous overtures.

The final dance was a passive one, with the dancing girls rotating on the stage and going to and fro, from one edge to the other, keeping to the increasing speed of the percussion instruments . . . The woman was gradually freed of her body . . . became pure movement, knelt and continued to rotate on her knees, faster and faster.

We had to turn our head continually to follow the moving spirit, the mirage . . . whirling incessantly . . . until the percussion abruptly reached a high point in loudness . . . and suddenly stopped . . . leaving the dancing girl fallen on the stage.

Entranced by the spectacle, we had forgotten the piercing, numbing cold. We returned to the train for sleep. It was after midnight. The wheels of the train began to move, slowly, to take us to the next stop.

Jodhpur
The Fortress City

Jodhpur, onetime capital of the principality of Marwar, lies two hundred kilometres east of Jaisalmer, on a shifting sandhill at the edge of the desert. Today, the remnants of an enormous rampart – eleven metres in periphery – with eight gateways, each facing a point of the compass, protect the city from the surrounding sands of the Thar desert. On the summit of the hill is the magnificent Mehrangarh fortress, built by Rao Jodha, in 1459, when he transferred his capital here from Mandore.

The sun was beginning to rise as we came out of the railway station and made our way towards the cars. Suddenly we saw a surprising sight, that made us stop in our tracks. In the midst of the usual seething mass of people going about their daily business, was a group of men . . . almost regimented, moving forward through the crowd . . . an army of workmen, their tools on their shoulders – picks, shovels, hammers, crowbars and buckets . . . that boarded the train, to be taken somewhere to repair the tracks.

As these men, or rather these spectres of men, advanced . . . they brought to our minds images of chain gangs . . . shrivelled, skinny, barefoot, ragged . . . they walked on to toil, up until nightfall, to earn a handful of rice and a morsel of bread, to keep them alive . . . in order to carry on the same, the next day. It was a sad picture, a negative picture in this country of contrasts.

We continued on our way to the fort-palace of Mehrangarh, which dominates the entire region. The closer we came to its towering vertical walls, the stronger was our impression of an impregnable stronghold. We negotiated the maze of narrow streets in the city and eventually arrived

Mehrangarh Durg

at the gate of this formidable fortress. The seven successive gates through which we passed were wrought of very strong iron with points, curves and metal designs, a complex that has a deterrent effect on all, even on battle elephants. We felt small and insignificant as we ascended the ramps between the high sheer walls, spare but solid.

The austere form of the fortress is in complete contrast to the refinement of the palace apartments. It is as if the architectural whole is dominated by a functional perception, in other words, the battlements were built to protect, while the apartments were intended for rest and relaxation.

Daulat Khana

We walked around and observed, marvelling at those who designed the structures, as well as at those anonymous masons who placed the stones, one by one, and bound them strongly together. Although this complex took generations to complete, we felt there was a sense of harmony. Windows overlooking atria and courtyards formed by the wings emphasise the unity of the architectural conception. Every window is protected by perforated stone screens in various lace-like patterns. Another feature of Mehrangarh is that it has far more women's apartments than men's – a clear indication that the princes of Jodhpur were more often on the field of battle than at home in the palace.

We roamed the halls and courtyards, climbing up and down staircases, admiring the wealth and the art adorning every surface. We saw the enormous traceried glass windows of the *Moti Mahal*, that cast polychrome patterns on the floor when the sun slips through the openings. In this charming women's apartment, the *maharanis* feasted and made merry.

As we wandered in the women's quarters we could feel for ourselves the kind of lives they had lived. The sumptuousness inside, secluded from the outside world – since the towering walls ruled out communication – gives you the impression of luxurious cages in which the female sex was confined . . . isolated from all other kinds of life, except strict devotion to husband and children. The culmination of the *maharanis*' devotion was *sati* – setting fire to oneself – when their menfolk were killed in the arena of war.

As we came down the stairs of the palace, we saw a memorial of such self-sacrifice. On a wall in the courtyard at the palace entrance are the imprints of many hands, of *maharanis* who committed *sati*. The only trace

Umaid Bhawan →

these women left of their passage through this life. A life they spent ... in luxury, but without the pleasures that are the birthright of every human being . . . seeing the sun rise, the stars sparkling in the sky, the flowers blossoming . . . feeling the cold of the desert and the warmth of the summer sun . . . being drenched in perspiration and cooling off in the shade of a tree, beside the running waters of a brook ... and even experiencing the thrill and heartthrob of love – that wonderful bounty – the supreme gift of life. You feel sorry for those women, who were born, grew up and died ... without really living, leaving their handprints on a wall, as the only trace of their life.

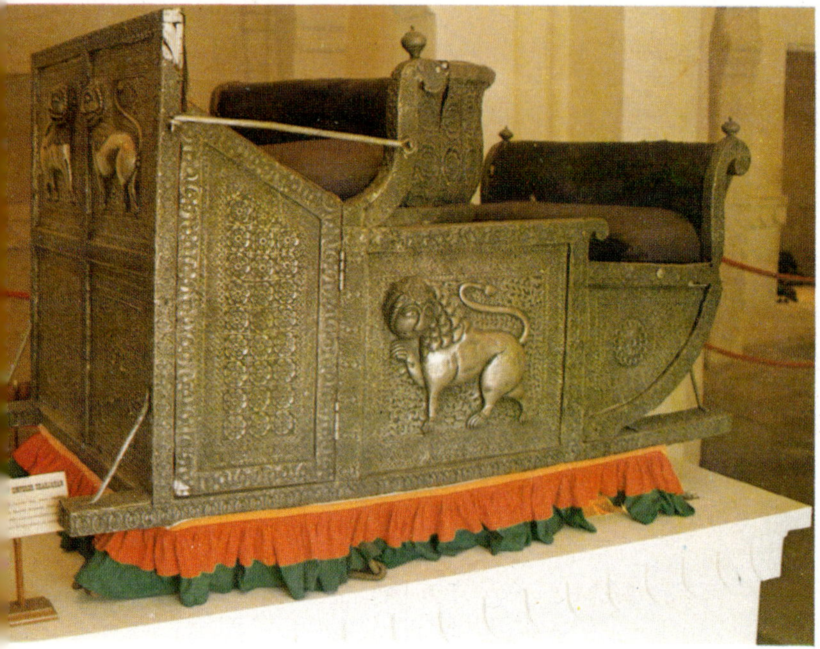

Haydah

Before leaving the fortress-palace, we clambered up onto a battlement, to enjoy the view . . . astonishing. The city spread out all around, with its little white houses, the blue homes of the brahmin ... and the serpentine streets ... And beyond, the plain on one side and the desert on the other, extending as far as the frontier and into Pakistan.

We went back down the corridors of the fortress, and into the car, to be driven to a modern palace, of the present *maharaja*.

On the way we stopped at a small knoll to see a building that is used as a crematorium ... for burning the dead ... with all the rites and respect customary in these parts.

Deval ↗

The Umaid Bhawan palace could be described as an exercise in rococo executed in solid, pinkish sandstone. It was built by the British architect H.U. Lanchester, whose previous experience had been with public buildings in his own country. It looks like a town hall converted into a palace.

Its grandeur is, I think, due more to its scale than anything else. We heard that three thousand workmen were employed on this project, and they laboured for fifteen years. A special branch of the railway line was laid to transport the blocks of sandstone over a distance of ten kilometres . . . in a region without water . . . in order to build a building – the present one – with a lift and air-conditioning, the first in India with these facilities. The palace also has large reception halls, conference halls, a spectacular roof with two domes, exhibition galleries and many other areas for different uses.

Jaswant Thada

The attempt to furnish it was disastrous. The furniture had been ordered from England during the Second World War. The ship carrying it to India was sunk by the Germans, while the factory in England was destroyed in the blitz. The result is a Hindu-Rajput palace with furniture and equipment that are, I would say, heavy and incongruous. Today the palace operates as a luxury hotel, in one part of which the *maharaja* of Jodhpur resides.

We had our lunch in this palace-hotel . . . and enjoyed the comfortable public rooms with all their lavish amenities. We looked at the museum collections of strange clocks and alarm clocks, displayed in special galleries together with antique porcelain . . . And eventually we lounged in the armchairs on the veranda, overlooking the garden . . . to pass the time until the train's departure for the next stop.

The garden of the palace-hotel, like all hotel gardens in India, is beautifully laid out and cared for, tended by teams of gardeners – labour is ridiculously cheap – who toil with zeal and patience, weeding, pruning and watering . . . to create a wonderful effect.

• • •

The next stop on our journey was Fatehpur Sikri, followed by Agra, cities we had visited leisurely – and which we have described in a previous chapter. But since they were included in the train's itinerary, we were delighted to be able to see them again.

We spent the day visiting and admiring the Taj Mahal and the fort of Agra again, wandering through the narrow streets of the city at leisure.

It is particularly pleasant to loiter at will, pausing when you want, whe. something catches your eye . . . perusing the diverse ornaments – so carefully and skilfully made – hung in the shops . . . smelling the aroma of the thousands of spices . . . gazing at the polychrome palette of powders used by the women for colouring the forehead, the cheeks . . . the eyes, to denote their status.

So we whiled away the day, gaining something different. As sunset drew near we went back to the train, to be taken to the end of our journey . . . Delhi, capital of India.

Gandhi-Nehru
The Founders of Modern India

I consider it necessary to insert this chapter, in order to present two personalities, the protagonists who set their seal on India's new course in the world: Gandhi and Nehru. Both utilised India's immense political and religious substratum, one which it had acquired over the centuries as the recipient of manifold external influences, and which it had the unique ability to absorb and assimilate into a synthesis that maintained its unity. This unity is not to be perceived as a force which standardised the various beliefs. It was something deeper that Gandhi and Nehru consolidated and transformed, giving the Indians the strength to struggle for liberation from colonialism, which was a serious danger to their country's single course.

One of modern India's greatest poets and thinkers, Rabindranath Tagore, said that:

> 'We have for over a century been dragged by the prosperous West behind its chariot, choked by the dust, deadened by the speed. We agreed to acknowledge that this chariot-drive was progress, and that progress was civilisation. If we ever ventured to ask "progress towards what, and

> progress for whom", it was considered to be peculiarly and ridiculously oriental to entertain such ideas about the absoluteness of progress. Of late, a voice has come to us bidding us to take count not only of the scientific perfection of the chariot but of the depth of the ditches lying across its path.'

India's problem at the beginning of the twentieth century was, on the one hand to gain independence, and on the other to choose the goals and values that would constitute the warp on which the social and ethnic weft of the new state would be woven. A state with an ancient and wonderful civilisation, which had to be transformed into an entity capable of asserting its own identity and of playing its role in the modern world. The basic contributors to this endeavour were Gandhi and Nehru, who gave India its present form. A form composed of, on the one hand, the elements of religion and culture since the time they were born and as they have been subsequently moulded under the influence of the many races that have, at various times, conquered and controlled the country in the course of its long history, and on the other, the elements it must assimilate from the modern world in order to play the role its enormous size and population impose.

India, after a long period of tumult and conquests by foreign invaders, began to lose its unity and its national entity, and to fall rapidly into decline. The climax of this was the formal confirmation of the dominance of colonialism, in 1858, when Queen Victoria assumed sovereignty of India and appointed the first Viceroy. British rule was consolidated and supported by British officials. The British irrigated some desert areas and improved communications. They worked for many years in India so that they felt more at home here than in their own country.

The British in India constituted the fifth caste, the first in the hierarchy. Superior to the brahmins and the kshatriyas. To them, all Indians were untouchables. They played the role of teachers who maintain silence in the classroom and teach the children to read and write, and to walk in a single file. In essence, however, they never taught the children anything that could help them find their own way.

The British were masters in a foreign house. Their presence was humiliating for the Indians. Every action, even of those few with the best of intentions, was a humiliation for the Indians. The British complained bitterly that the Indians were 'ungrateful'. Their complaints were a measure of their lack of understanding. The British failed to decipher the profundity of the essence that was India. India was for them a weak, dirty, backward country with a few lovely monuments and some splendid minds, but in general inferior and Asian.

Even if the British had changed India into a land flowing with milk and honey, they would still have been an anathema. Colonialism, like dictatorship, burns the soul, debases the spirit and diminishes the individual, however well it rules. Its allies are fear and cowardice. Colonialism is the government of other peoples, by other peoples, for other peoples. Whatever the subjects gain, however significant this is, it is no more than the by-product of their efforts on behalf of their distant Masters.

The demands of British prestige hurt Indian pride. All the visible manifestations of the British regime – the magnificent ceremonies, the secluded settlements and the villas in which the British lived, and even the use of the English language – told the Indians they were a vassal race.

Subjugation stimulates the desire for liberation.

This is the reason why colonial administration never was and never will be successful. There are no good colonial powers in history. Every empire digs its own grave. Colonialism is a constant hybris because it considers that foreigners, outsiders, have the right to govern the insiders, the locals, who are not fit to govern themselves. It is this which inevitably creates the opposite, Nationalism.

Gandhi

It was in this period and this milieu that Mohandas Karamchand Gandhi appeared, who embodied and gave meaning to Indian nationalism. He was the herald of non-violence in the twentieth century. Gandhi was not an opponent who used the means we are used to, war aimed at bringing the adversary violently to his knees. He himself, with his behaviour, set the example. His personality evolved through hard struggles he waged in order to first form his character, through an attempt at exercise.

Mohandas Gandhi was born on 2 October 1869 at Porbandar, capital of the small principality of Gujarat. He belonged to the vaishya caste, which is slightly lower in the hierarchy than the brahmins and the kshatriyas – the caste of governors and warriors – and a little above the shudras, the caste of labourers. The Gandhi family belonged to the Bania subdivision of their caste. Bania in India is synonymous with the wily trader and the Gandhi, family were, at one time, grocers – which is what the word Gandhi, means. When, as years passed, the professional barriers between the castes began to be relaxed, the Gandhis started becoming involved in politics and the problems of the region in which they lived. Gandhi's father was for a period prime minister in one of the small principalities. Mohandas wrote: 'My father had no education other than what experience had taught him. He was "innocent" of history and geography, but he was incorruptible and had gained the respect of society for his just behaviour.' He married four times.

Mohandas Gandhi was the fourth child of his father's fourth marriage. His mother, Putlibai, was deeply religious and Mohandas grew up in a household devoted to Vaishnavism – the worship of the god Vishnu – and deeply influenced by Jainism, which denied violence. Thus, for him, not causing harm to a living creature, fasting for purification, and tolerance among the devotees of the various religions and sects were natural, self-evident imperatives.

In his youth he was average in performance. He was not an attractive-looking boy, but he had the ardent desire to improve himself, taking as models of life even the heroes of Indian mythology, incarnations of honesty and sacrifice. His parents married him off at the age of thirteen . . . and decided to send him to England, in order that he acquire the necessary education to become a lawyer, so that he could claim a high position in one of the principalities of Gujarat.

Gandhi was enthusiastic. In his youthful imagination England was the land 'of philosophers and poets, the very centre of civilisation'.

His studies in England were a turning point in his life. His passage from the semi-rural environment of India to the cosmopolitan life of London was not easy. Everyday he experienced situations which forged his character and formed his personality. He had met various people, a hotch-potch of vegetarians, socialists, humanists and theosophists, idealists and revolutionaries who rejected the established values of the late Victorian era, denounced the wounds of capitalism and industrial society, eulogised the simple life and professed that moral values are superior to material ones, collaboration preferable to conflict.

When Mohandas returned to India in 1891 he discovered that his Law degree did not automatically guarantee him a profitable career. After a succession of professional failures he was relieved to sign a contract with an Indian firm in Natal, South Africa.

• • •

Gandhi's sojourn in Africa proved catalytic for the formation of his character. There he saw and experienced injustice and apartheid in its fullest expression. In a court in Durban the judge asked him to remove his turban. He refused and left the chamber. One day he was forcibly removed from a first-class railway carriage. On another occasion a bus-driver beat him up because he refused to give his seat to a white man. In Pretoria he could not find a hotel to stay in, because they were all for 'Europeans only'.

Humiliations such as these were everyday occurrences for the Indian tradesmen and labourers in Natal, who were used to them and accepted them with forbearance. For Gandhi, however, it was the moment of truth. Of truth that made manifest his conviction that he would no longer accept the injustice that prevailed in South Africa and would defend his dignity as an Indian and as a man.

So Gandhi, who had not read a newspaper until he was eighteen and who was indifferent to politics until he was twenty-five, suddenly became an experienced activist. He compiled a memorandum for the legislative body of Natal, which he got hundreds of his compatriots to sign, and began a struggle for the rights of all citizens. He settled in Durban, in order to practise as a barrister and to organise the Indian community. He founded the Indian Congress Party of Natal and through it managed to inculcate the spirit of solidarity in the Indian community.

Gandhi's name came to be known outside South Africa. In Britain public opinion began to be aware of, and to protest against, the sufferings of Indians in Natal. On the contrary, the European population of Natal was enraged.

So, in 1897, when Gandhi returned to Durban after a trip to India to bring over his wife, Kasturbabai, and their children, he was practically lynched by a gang of whites. Typical of Gandhi's behaviour was that he did not press charges against the perpetrators because, as he said, it was not his principle to prosecute those who had wronged him personally.

Gandhi was not vindictive. In the Boer War, in 1899, he set up a corps of stretcher-bearers from thousands of Indian volunteers, because he believed that since they were demanding full political rights in the colony of Natal, they had an obligation to stand by the side of the British crown and serve those whom they regarded as tyrants.

In 1906 the government of the Transvaal published a humiliating decree for preparing a census of the Indian population. The Indians, headed by Gandhi, swore to defy the decree if it were implemented despite their protest. Thus the *satyagraha* (devotion to truth) was born, a new tactic according to which one should demand reparation of injustice done not by causing pain, but through resisting the opponent without hatred and fighting him without violence.

The struggle with this tactic lasted seven years. Many Indians preferred to give up their bread and liberty, rather than to submit to laws contrary to their conscience and their self-respect. Hundreds of Indians, men and women, were put in gaol and thousands of Indian workers who went on strike in the mines courageously faced imprisonment, torture and the firing squad. This was the worst possible 'publicity' for the South African government, which eventually agreed to proceed to a compromise solution with negotiations between Gandhi on one side and the South African public figure, General Jan Christian Smuts on the other.

South Africa treated Gandhi harshly, drawing him into the vortex of the racial problem, but it offered him the ideal field in which to develop his singular qualities.

• • •

In 1915, after a short stay in England, Gandhi returned to India. Alone and independent, he avoided all involvement in political mobilisations. He struggled to keep an open mind, reserving the right to different opinions. His life, as he himself said, was one long experiment. For him nothing was predestined. He was independent, noncommital, indefinable and consequently difficult. A discussion with Gandhi was a journey of exploration. He dared to go anywhere without a map. He was attacked and he rarely defended himself. Humble and simple, attuned to India, he condemned no one. He did not say or do anything to gain publicity or to acquire followers.

Gandhi helped the British in the First World War, even recruiting men into the British army in India. But at the same time he did not hesitate to criticise the British for tyrannical acts or to stand by the farmers of Bihar and Gujarat. The British insistence on promoting legislation authorising imprisonment without trial (suspension of habeas corpus) of those suspected of sedition, brought Gandhi for the first time into open breach with the colonial power. He declared a *satyagraha* struggle. The result was a veritable earthquake which shook the Indian peninsula in the spring of 1919. The violent clashes that followed, and which were the pretext for the massacre of some four hundred Indians by the British soldiers at Amritsar in the Punjab, forced Gandhi to stop the struggle. The outcry of the Indians roused Gandhi's fighting spirit again.

By the autumn of 1920 Gandhi was the dominant figure in India, exercising an influence unprecedented for an Indian leader. He transformed the National Congress Party into a mass political organisation whose tentacles spread to even the smallest village. Gandhi's message was clear and simple: it was not the British guns that were keeping the country enslaved, but the flaws of the Indians themselves.

The programme of non-violence and non-cooperation with everything directly or indirectly connected with the British electrified the atmosphere, dispelled the fear in the face of the foreign power and led thousands of Indians, who resolutely joined the queue, to be locked up in gaol. Gandhi was arrested, tried for sedition and sentenced to six years' imprisonment.

Unfortunately, however, the existence of one important man does not mean the existence of others who can continue the same course on their own. Various contending factions emerged in the Congress Party because petty interests overruled the dominant issue. Gandhi reacted by going on a hunger strike, in order to be heard favourably by the people and to continue the way of non-violence.

In December 1928 Gandhi demanded that the British Government grant autonomy within a year, under the threat of a pan-Indian, non-violent campaign for the country's full independence, and once more assumed the leadership of the Congress Party. In March 1930 he replied with *satyagraha* following the imposition of the tax on salt, which hit the poorer classes. This was one of his most sucessful campaigns in the non-violent struggle against the British, that resulted in the imprisonment of sixty thousand people.

The British Government decided to estrange Gandhi from the outside world and annihilate his influence. To this end they imprisoned him in 1931. But he continued his struggle from gaol. A decision to isolate the 'untouchables' with the separate elctoral wards provided for in the new constitution, triggered off another hunger strike by Gandhi, signalling the start of a dynamic campaign for the rehabilitation of the untouchables, whom Gandhi renamed *Harijans* (children of God).

In 1934 Gandhi resigned his leadership and membership of the Congress Party, because he believed that its prominent members had adopted the doctrine of non-violence for reasons of political expediency and not out of conviction, as he had.

He devoted himself to the reconstitution of the nation 'from the foundation'. He educated the peasants who constituted 85 per cent of the population, continued the struggle for the inclusion of the pariahs in the social whole and encouraged various cottage industries such as spinning and weaving which would enable the underemployed to supplement their income. In parallel, he designed an educational system that met the needs of the people.

The Second World War proved decisive for developments in India. Gandhi hated fascism and all that it represented, but he also hated war. He returned to active politics. The British were not prepared to promise anything positive regarding the handing over of power to the Indians, and cultivated the climate of dissension between Muslims and Hindus. In the most critical period of the war against the Axis, in 1942, the British reacted violently, imprisoning the entire leadership of the Congress Party. Popular indignation was expressed in ugly insurrections which were mercilessly crushed. The rift between the British and the Indians was wider than ever before.

A new chapter in British-Indian relations opened with the victory of the Labour Party in Britain, in the 1945 elections. Long negotiations ended in the Mountbatten plan, which made provision for the setting up of the self-governing states of India and Pakistan.

One of Gandhi's greatest disappointments was that India had achieved its freedom at the loss of its unity. The separatist movement had created a climate of continual strife between Muslims and Hindus. All that remained for Gandhi was to concern himself with healing the wounds the religious enmity had inflicted.

In this atmosphere charged with hatred and suspicion Gandhi's task was difficult and disagreeable. He was accused by the supporters of both factions. And when he did not gain anything by persuasion, he resorted to fasting. So he stopped the bloody clashes in Calcutta and shamed the religious rivals into calling a truce. A few days later, on 30 January 1948, while Gandhi was going to his place of evening prayer in Delhi, he was assassinated by a Hindu fanatic.

• • •

Lord Mountbatten – the last Viceroy of India – speaking on how Gandhi was regarded in India, said:

> 'They do not compare him with some of the great political leaders, such as Churchill or Roosevelt. They place him in their mind alongside Mohammed and Christ. Millions worship Mahatma, a host tries to kiss his feet or the dust from his footprints. They respect him and reject his teaching. They consider his person sacred and desecrate his personality. They praise the shell and trample the essence. They believe in him, but not in his principles.'

Gandhi was a great peacemaker and reconciler, between the old conservatives and the young radicals, the terrorists and the parliamentarians, the urban intellectuals and the rural masses, the fiduciaries of tradition and the innovators, the Hindu castes and the untouchables, the Indians and the British.

His motives should be sought in religion and not in politics. Religion for him did not mean formal observance, dogma, ritual or heterodoxy. 'That which I have struggled and suffered to achieve in these thirty years', he wrote in his autobiography, 'is to see God face to face'. But in order to do this he did not withdraw to a cave in the Himalayas, seeking the Absolute, like many of his compatriots. He carried his cave inside him. He believed that no one discovers truth shut up within the narrow confines of his personal life, but in the arena of social and political life.

For millions of his fellow Indians Gandhi was the *Mahatma* (the great soul). The spontaneous worship of the crowd that thronged and jostled to see him from one end of his route to the other made his tours difficult and prevented him from working by day and sleeping at night. 'Only the Mahatmas know the torments of the Mahatmas', he wrote.

Mahatma Gandhi was the catalyst, if not the fuse, of three of the most important revolutions in the twentieth century: the revolutions against colonialism, racial discrimination and violence.

Nehru

Unlike Gandhi, who was of petit bourgeois origins, Nehru was the scion of an aristocratic brahmin family from Kashmir, famed for its administrative abilities and learning, that had migrated to India in the early eighteenth century.

Jawaharlal Nehru was born on 14 November 1880 at Allahabad. His father, Motilal Nehru was an eminent lawyer and one of the most important representatives of Mahatma Gandhi. Indulged as a child, Jawaharlal was raised in the lap of luxury, in a house with its own swimming pool and tennis court, and educated by English governesses and private tutors.

In 1905 he entered Harrow, one of Britain's top public schools, which he attended for two years. He went on to study at Trinity College, Cambridge, graduating in the Physical Sciences. After Cambridge he trained as a barrister at the Inner Temple. Four years after his return to India, in March 1916, he married Kamala Kaul, the daughter of a family originating from Kashmir. Their only child, Indira Priyadarshini, was born in 1917. She too was destined to become prime minister of India, as Indira Gandhi (after her marriage).

When he returned to India, Nehru went into practice as a lawyer. However, his belief that he should help the liberation of his country led him into politics. When he and his father met Gandhi they were persuaded to follow his policy. The characteristic of Gandhi that impressed both the Nehrus was his insistence on action.

Mahatma said an evil should not just be condemned; it should be resisted.

Nehru's association with the Congress Party began in 1919, the year of the massacre at Amritsar in April, when the British military commander ordered the army to open fire on an assembled crowd of unarmed Indians. In 1921 Nehru was imprisoned for the first time. In 1921 he became general secretary of the party for two years, and again in 1927 for two years.

Though Nehru was vaguely drawn towards Socialism, his Radicalism was confused. A trip to Europe and the Soviet Union in 1926-27 had a seminal effect on clarifying his thinking. Although he only visited Russia for a few days, and he was conscious that he saw only what he was allowed to see, he was impressed by the rapid progress made in agriculture, fighting illiteracy, handling the problems of minorities and neutralising the antithesis between luxury and poverty in the class hierarchy. He was also sure that the Soviet Union would have much to teach India, a rural country with a poor and illiterate population.

Nehru saw the Soviet Union in the last of its halcyon days. If his reaction was idealistic this is also due to the general atmosphere in Europe at the time concerning Marxism. Nehru, who left India a devoted disciple of Gandhi, returned a convinced, revolutionary radical. Although he remained deeply influenced by Gandhi, he was no longer totally given to the model his mentor had created. Jawaharlal was always a radical in the European tradition, seeking to apply and adopt its doctrines to his country. This was at once a strength and a weakness.

After the Lahore convention in 1929, Nehru emerged as a leader of the intellectuals and young people of India. Gandhi, in the hope that Nehru would draw the youth of India – at that time tending to extreme leftism – into the mainstream of the Congress movement, cleverly promoted him to the presidency of the Congress Party, over the head of many of his seniors. Mahatma had calculated correctly that, with this additional responsibility, Nehru himself would be obliged to follow the middle way.

After the death of his father in 1931, Nehru was promoted to the internal councils of the Congress Party and became more closely attached to Mahatma. Although Gandhi did not officially designate him as his political successor until 1942, India had seen in the person of Nehru, from as early as 1930, Gandhi's natural successor.

The Gandhi-Irwin accord established a truce between the Indians and the British, after the movement of disobedience. There followed consultations in London on the possibility of self-government for India, which finally resulted in the 1935 India Home Rule Act that ceded to the Indian provinces a system of popular autonomous government and guaranteed a federal system in which the autonomous provinces and principalities would participate. In the end, only the provincial autonomy was applied.

In the mid-1930s developments in Europe indicated it was heading for a new world war. Nehru stressed that in the event of war India would be on the side of the democracies, though he insisted that India could only fight alongside Great Britian and France as a free state.

In the ensuing elections for provincial autonomy, the Congress Party was brought to power in most of the provinces. Nehru was on the horns of a dilemma. The Muslim League, led by Mohammed Ali Jinnah (the founder of Pakistan), had not done well in the elections. Congress rejected Jinnah's request to form coalition governments between the Congress Party and the Muslim League in some provinces, a decision for which Nehru bore much of the responsibility.

The conflict which followed developed into a vicious dispute between Hindus and Muslims, and led eventually to the partition of India and the creation of Pakistan.

• • •

Nehru's opinions on the war differed from those of Gandhi, who believed that the British should be helped, without terms but also without violence. Nehru maintained that non-violence could not be effective against an armed attack and that India could help Great Britain in the war against Nazism only as an independent country.

The two men also differed in their approach to the issue of independence. While Gandhi refused to accept the division of India into two states, Nehru reluctantly but realistically agreed to their creation. On 15 August 1947 India and Pakistan appeared as two independent countries. Nehru was the first prime minister of India.

In the thirty-five years since 1929, when Gandhi chose him as president of the convention of the Congress Party in Lahore, until his death as prime minister in 1964, Nehru remained – despite the utter collapse India suffered at the hands of the Chinese in 1962 – the idol of his people.

Superficially, his secular approach to politics was in contrast to the religious and traditional stance of Gandhi, which had erroneously given Indian politics a religious mould, since Gandhi, although he could be considered a pious conservative, was in reality a social non-conformist who strove to secularise Hinduism.

The real difference between Nehru and Gandhi did not lie in their attitude to religion, but in their attitude to civilisation. While Nehru spoke an increasingly modern language, Gandhi returned to the glories of ancient India. And yet, within the context of Hinduism, Gandhi was, from the social viewpoint, as much a protestant as Nehru was outside it.

Gandhi and Nehru complemented one another and revealed an internal unity which represents enduring truths and has a perpetual quality for the good of mankind. Dr. Shanker Dayal Sharma, the current President of the Republic of India, describes Gandhi as a 'saintly revolutionary' and Nehru as a 'revolutionary architect'. This is apparent in their description of each other. Gandhi spoke of Nehru as 'clear as crystal', defining him as the 'chosen instrument' of God. Gandhi said prophetically of Nehru: 'When I leave, he will speak my language. When I no longer exist, he will continue my work'. And Nehru said of Gandhi: 'Perhaps he is the greatest symbol of India of the past and he will be, I say, the symbol of the future'.

The inner light of Gandhi's and Nehru's thinking was created from the very values intensely preserved by both of them and which determined the personal and combined form of their energy. Both together personified the dynamic realisation of these values: Truth, Non-violence, Tolerance and Understanding, Peace, Cooperation and Friendship, Care and Sacrifice, which constitute the nucleus of the ideas and the debt crystallised in the moral values of which Mahatma Gandhi and Jawaharlal Nehru were expressors and possessors.

It is important for us to appreciate that belief in the supremacy of moral values, of non-violence, peace, friendship and cooperation, is a vision for the evolution of the human race. It encompasses a philosophy and an attitude to life, of Gandhi and Nehru, in an era when the world has been flooded by immense waves of hatred and violence.

In a blood-stained period of history, when war and death wiped out millions of people in a darkness that covered all, the thinking of Gandhi and Nehru gave tremendous significance to the history of human thought. Their philosophy was a solitary but splendid light which dispelled the darkness and kept alive hope for mankind.

• • •

Nehru's importance in the perspective of Indian history is that he introduced and disseminated many Western values and ways of thinking he considered useful for India. He separated the state from religion and the unity of India, despite its lack of racial and religious homogeneity. Nehru tried and managed to lead India into the modern age of scientific discoveries and technological development.

Characteristic is Nehru's reply to Mountbatten, last Viceroy of India, when asked: 'What is the greatest problem facing India?'. His answer was 'the economic problem', because he believed that democracy cannot be founded upon social injustice and poverty. This was one of his first concerns. He awakened the people, making them aware of the need for social welfare for the poor and the pariahs, and the need for respect of democratic values. One of the achievements of which he was particularly proud was the reform of the ancient Indian code, that allowed, at last, in Hindu lands, women to be treated as equals of men in matters of inheritance and property.

Nehru was only one of the leaders of the Congress Party, including Gandhi, who had thought seriously about India's place in the world community. If Gandhi made the Indians aware of the others, when India achieved its independence, the image it presented to the world was, in reality, the image of Nehru.

Delhi
The Glorious Capital

Delhi, located in the centre of northern India, was the crossroads through which the invaders of the subcontinent were obliged to pass.

Many of these conquerors chose it as their capital – initially, various Indian and Muslim dynasties, subsequently the mighty Mughals, the British, and finally the Indians when India gained its Independence.

In the last four hundred and fifty years, this city has been the capital of India eight times, developing according to the peoples living here. That is why the growth of Delhi – in contrast to the other large cities of India, the ports of Bombay and Madras, and Calcutta with its mud dwellings – has been ambitious in its prospects for at least four-and-a-half centuries.

Countless monuments, including the tombs and mausoleums of eighteen emperors, endow the city with a cultural heritage. Even the place of Gandhi's cremation is here.

This concentration of monuments in Delhi, which number over one thousand, dates back to the end of the twelfth century, when the Afghan

Qutb-ud-din-Aibek was declared Sultan and created the Sultanate of Delhi. After him came various rulers – until, in 1526, Babur, the first great Mughal, transferred his capital from Delhi to Agra. There it remained until Shah Jahan came to power in 1650, and once more made Delhi capital of his empire. This Mughal emperor, who had a penchant for art and a partiality for architecture, created the seventh city – remnants of which still survive in Old Delhi – and initiated the renaissance of Delhi. But Shah Jahan's reign was fated to be short. In 1658 his son, Aurangzeb, who feared the conspiracies of the throne, imprisoned his father in the fort at Agra, where he died. At first Aurangzeb wanted to confine his father elsewhere, but Shah Jahan preferred the fort at Agra from where, through a mirror, he could see the Taj Mahal. Twenty years later, Aurangzeb abandoned Delhi and transferred his capital to the Deccan . . . from where he could conduct his military campaigns more easily.

Aurangzeb's withdrawal marked the beginning of Delhi's decline. It was successively captured and plundered by Persians and Afghans. Chaos prevailed and continued until 1803, when Delhi fell into British hands.

In 1911 the British monarch, King George V, announced the transfer of the capital of India to Delhi once more. Following this decision, distinguished British architects began to plan the new capital city, New Delhi. A grand urban centre with palatial buildings set beside broad avenues and Mughal-style gardens, complemented by fountains and lakes.

The British architect Sir Edwin Lutyens wanted to revet the façades of the edifices with marble, but for reasons of economy, sandstone was used as the main material instead. Within twenty years the building of the capital was finished.

However, the British did not manage to complete the decoration of the enormous interiors, since they were obliged to leave. India gained its independence, and the imperial city designed and completed by the British nowadays serves the native leaders of the young republic.

In the years that have passed since the liberation of India, Delhi has grown at a rapid pace, and now has a population of over nine million. As a consequence of this growth, the two adjacent cities, Old and New Delhi, have been united into one . . . which continues to retain its two sides.

When the train reached Delhi it was already morning. A mist had blanketed everything. We could barely see anything. The train chugged along slowly. Visibility was so low that we were obliged to wait – even after we had arrived – for the heavy cloud covering the streets, houses . . . and people, to clear.

We were quite late in reaching the hotel . . . a most luxurious building at the edge of the city, in a beautifully laid-out area where the foreign embassies and the residence of diplomats are located.

We settled in our rooms . . . and enjoyed . . . the water, which we had missed . . . and the comfort we sought after being constantly on the move for so long . . . visiting the many cities and regions of India, that I have tried to describe in this book.

We also had to sort out our collected experiences. We needed to talk with Indians, in order to verify our experiences and to see whether our

The Red Fort

The India Gate

reflections, a result of judgement . . . on the thought-provoking information given to us by the land itself . . . the continual pounding of the mind and the senses . . . were on the right course. Such questions cannot be answered by a simple yes or no . . . especially when this country's ancient civilisation, moulded by a host of outside influences, has created an environment in which modern man is trying to find his way . . . under objectively difficult conditions in comparison with the Western world.

We devoted the day to meetings with Indians, with persons who can express and signal developments in the immediate and distant future.

At noon I visited Dr. Shankar Dayal Sharma, the President of the Indian Republic, in the presidential palace, a splendid building erected by the British, dominating the broad avenues of New Delhi. Officials led me through a succession of corridors and halls, to a waiting room. A few minutes later I was ushered into an audience chamber – totally different from those we had encountered in the palaces of the Mughal emperors – where Dr. Sharma was waiting for me. A modest, mature man . . . fully aware of what he is seeking, humane and with a breadth of experience, acquired in his service alongside Nehru and his many years of activity as a politician and philosopher. He inspires respect . . . as a leader who does not acquire prestige from his position but whose personality gives prestige to the highest office he holds. I had been fortunate in meeting him some six months back, in Athens . . . and had enjoyed the maturity of his thinking . . . the distillate of education, tradition, his experience of life and the cultivation of his soul. He is a leader who is very different from the leaders we are used to meeting from the West . . . Men whose ambition and power to achieve their goal, by any means, undeniably bespeaks a strong

Raj-path and the presidential house

personality, but deprives them . . . of the humane element, which is the essential and unique means that can guide them to choose . . . human solutions to the problems they confront.

After a short but stimulating discussion with him, I said goodbye . . . sure that . . . as far as it is within his power, he will strive to utilise the advantages offered by Western technology. Advantages that will aid India's development and infrastructure – without entailing a change in its orientation, in the tradition and the way of life that the Indians have chosen, as individuals and as a state.

As I was returning to the hotel, crossing the avenues of Delhi, I was thinking and dreaming, at the same time, of the potential this country of eight hundred and fifty million people (one-fifth of the present population of the planet) has . . . to propose for the future another way of life . . . with simple, humane societies that have ranked their goals . . . according to some criteria aimed at happiness. A ranking asserting the internal development and maturing of individuals, and not the frantic, irrational pursuit of wealth and the sole supremacy of the senses. A ranking like that of the ancient Greeks, who reconciled the absolute order of logic with the vital, sweeping power of the senses. So, here, India could transmit another message . . . propose another way of life, capable of leading mankind into the third millennium AD.

In the hotel lobby, O.P. Jain was waiting for me. An Indian dressed in elements of native costume. A man who, having voluntarily ended an entrepreneurial career, in which he made a lot of money, has decided to spend the rest of his life . . . serving his country by enhancing its cultural

(Side) *Qutub Minar*
(below) *details*

identity. For this purpose he has set up a non-profit-making foundation that restores palaces and converts them info hotels . . . plans exhibitions . . . and has built a village outside Delhi. A place where artists and craftsmen meet and work . . . in traditional techniques, so as to ensure firm foundations of tradition in this land. He invited us to visit the village the next day. An invitation we were delighted to accept.

The third meeting that day was with a lady whose father was Indian and mother Greek . . . a member of a family which now plays an important role in the economic development of India. This meeting, apart from giving me the opportunity of getting to know this section of Indian society, gave us a hostess-guide to Delhi during our stay there.

So that evening we strolled through the streets and neighbourhoods of Delhi . . . ending up at Connaught Circus – an enormous circular area in the city centre, with a host of shops filled with people going in and out, buying and selling. It was late indeed when we returned to the hotel . . . to sleep, in order to set off the following day for the tour of the city.

Our tour commenced from south Delhi . . . with the *Qutb Minar*, a round tower seventy-three metres high, the construction of which began in 1200, by Qutb-ud-din Aibek, after his capture of Delhi. It continued with the addition of four more storeys by his son-in-law and heir. Later, in the fourteenth century, Firoz Shah Tughlak, in his efforts to rectify some obvious damage, repaired the tower . . . destroying its harmonious lines. He added further height and marble to the top two storeys, giving the building a heavy aspect.

We stopped quite some distance from the archaeological site and walked in the serene, verdant landscape. The tower dominated the region, drawing all attention to it. Only when we were really close did we become aware of the complex of buildings covering the site. Next to the base of the tower is a mosque, the first Muslim place of worship built in India, in the twelfth century, after the victory of the Muslims . . . over the Chauhan dynasty.

The Muslims used their victory to spread the tenets of Islam. And to show their superiority over the natives, they built their mosque next to a Hindu temple, using material – particularly columns – from twenty-seven Indian shrines. This explains why you can see Hindu and Jain sculptures in various parts of the mosque.

We had a good look at the different parts of the ruined mosque, its walls and openings. Close by rises an iron column, eight metres high, incised with Sanskrit inscriptions. This column, dated to the fifth century, originally stood in front of a temple dedicated to Vishnu. It was moved to its present position in the eleventh century. What is strange is that though of iron, it has not rusted . . . in all these years. Legend has it that if you stand with your back against the column, put your arms around it and embrace it, all your wishes will come true. Some of the ladies in our party tried . . . their luck. I don't know what they wished . . . or whether it has come true . . . There is, I think, no temporal horizon for such things. It is just an opportunity for one to hope . . . and it is hope which gives life and courage.

After walking on a little further, westwards, we stopped in front of another building . . . another tower, this one twenty-seven metres high. Although intended to be twice as high as the *Qutb Minar*, it remained half-finished because Allah-ud-din, who began it, died . . . and no-one could continue the work. A work of arrogance and immoderation . . . such as was, is and will be found as long as there are men on this planet . . . For most of the time man forgets who he is and tries to achieve the impossible.

Just beyond the mosque is the tomb of the emperor Iltutmish, the earliest tomb of a Muslim ruler in Delhi. Without roof, it seems discordant . . . or perhaps it complements the ruins . . . anyhow, it reminds us of the people who came here and trod this earth and gave a different direction to the history of India.

Jain Temple near Redfort

We wandered about a little longer, along the passages and in the open areas created by the walls, the trees and the flowers . . . full of a feeling of curiosity and contemplation . . . until we got back into the cars to be driven to the village of our friend O.P. Jain.

O.P. Jain's village is located outside Delhi, on the border of Haryana state, in a rural area with rich vegetation. As soon as we entered the fenced-off area we were faced by an orderly grid of lovely little houses, built of the familiar pinkish sandstone and with tiled roofs. The type of houses defined their various functions. Workshops for pottery, copper- and silver-smithing, in which handmade objects of folk art are produced . . . by craftsmen working in the very same way as their forefathers, moulding clay and hammering metal. Their creations are displayed in a spacious museum, where specialist scholars classify them according to region and date . . . so that the visitor can gain a correct picture of the differences between the regions of India and comprehend the chronological development.

← *A shop in Kinari Bazar*

The larger statues are placed in the courtyards round the houses which, together with other outdoor areas, create a peaceful and pleasant environment for the visitor . . . who, after the tour of the workshops and museum, can sit in comfortable chairs or on benches arranged for his convenience.

A row of houses a little beyond is for the artists – poets, painters, musicians and writers – to live and work in creativity, without distraction.

Artificial streams flowing through the village are an additional attractive feature . . . creating a man-made natural grove in which one can stroll, sit and think . . . far away from the bustle of the city, from current events . . . to be immersed in the work he is creating . . . and to offer it to the India of tomorrow.

There is even a small theatre for exercises and performances, as well as for rehearsing the endless diversity of dance movements.

We ate lunch in the garden, beside the trees, looking at these lovely buildings and watching the movement of the craftsmen, who work incessantly. We chatted for a while . . . listening mainly to the intentions and plans of the village's creator . . . a man of passion and quality, who has essentially devoted his life to the cultural development of his homeland. An action that is an affirmation not a negation, and which, I believe, it is imperative should be emulated by as many as possible . . . in all parts of the world . . . For the hope of a better world can only be based on man's elevation through education. Knowledge of history and knowledge of today's scientific achievements, in the correct mixture, will give that balance and measure of life on which and only by which a better world can be founded.

It was dusk when we got back to the hotel, our minds full of thoughts and impressions, which prompted questions . . . that must be answered some time.

We woke early the next day, for our schedule was heavy. We had to visit the National Museum, and as much of the city as possible.

The National Museum is a plain building, but absolutely functional. It is a treasure trove of works of art, well exhibited, giving the visitor a good idea of the history and art of India. Collections of precious objects from the Indies and Central Asia. Art and archaeology, anthropology, the decorative arts and textiles are represented harmoniously in its galleries. There is a wealth of prehistoric finds (5000 BC) from the Indus valley, as well as of Brahman, Jain and Buddhist statues of stone, bronze and clay. Other galleries house manuscripts, many of them penned in gold ink and illuminated with miniatures depicting persons and scenes described in the texts.

You could spend days and days, examining, comparing and cross-linking the exhibits with what you have read and the impressions gained in the course of the journey. Alas, we are always saying the same phrase . . . you could! Life is short, and those who are not specialist scholars must be content with the fragrance of what they see.

We continued our tour in the imperial city, modern Delhi, from the Arch of India, India Gate, built to honour the Indians killed in the First World War. The names of ninety thousand Indians who lost their life in the Great War are incised on the arch.

The imperial Rajpath Avenue – the widest thoroughfare in the city –

where Independence Day is celebrated annually on 26 January, runs westwards. To the right and left stand huge, splendid buildings, with thousands of rooms and countless corridors, housing ministries. A little behind is the Parliament building, a circular edifice of red and grey stone with open colonnades around the entire circumference. It houses both Chambers of Parliament, the House of the People and the Council of States. Next to it is the Presidential Palace I had visited earlier.

We also visited a hospital, opposite the Red Fort. Not an ordinary hospital for sick people, but a hospital for birds, run for several decades now by the Jains. The herbivorous birds – and rabbits – are nursed in the building, while the birds and animals that are not herbivorous are tended in the courtyards. The problem is that the birds that are cured are reluctant to leave. So the hospital can easily be located from the flocks of birds flying above it.

That afternoon we were invited for tea at the house of the in-laws of our Indo-Greek friend, who had been our guide the past few

Birla temple →

days. It was a visit that gave us the chance to meet people from the world of business, who are helping establish the economic future of this country. A country with a small industrial infrastructure, which though with a rich subsoil, is only now beginning to plan and to take the first steps towards its development. Essential to the success of this endeavour is the contribution of a significant proportion of scientists, who have studied in India and abroad and are trying to apply the basic theories of modern management in the development of industry and trade.

The house we visited combined modern amenities with tradition. A spacious sitting room with chairs round the edge and a few choice works of Indian art – bronze statues, miniatures and carpets – defining the status of the owners. Our hosts, all gathered *en famille* – the men in dark European suits and the women in Indian *saris* – received us with dignity and solemnity.

They offered us tea and we talked about the problems, the prospects, the hopes and dreams . . . with regard to their efforts, but particularly and primarily with regard to India, which constitutes the first priority in all their choices. Industrialists of several generations now, they continue the tradition, with their children, diversifying their interest into other sectors – chemicals, sugar refining, fertilisers, machines . . . and recently motor cars. They maintain a hierarchy in which each is obliged to keep the unwritten laws established by tradition. In their endeavour they use young scientists, who work as a team for the development of their project.

As the discussion digressed into other spheres, we further ascertained a replete maturity in their view of life and of man's role in it, in which the ranking of goals is not aimed at the acquisition of personal wealth, but at the development of their activities, dependent on which is their contribution to the general development of India.

It was late evening when we said goodbye to these mature, unaffected people, with a feeling of satisfaction and love for this country, that is advancing slowly but steadily along the right path.

We went to bed early since our next day in Delhi was to be the last in India . . . and we had to make the most of it, to reap as much as we possibly could.

The Parting Hours

The End of a Romance

← *Chandni chowk*

It was our last day in India, the end of our journey. The sun was shining in the bright blue sky and nature was clad in its Sunday best to bid us farewell.

We crossed the wide avenues, passed through the Arch of India, and there, before us, rose the solid mass of the Red Fort. This fort, that takes its name from the colour of the stone with which it is built, is the symbol of Shah Jahan, the symbol of Mughal might and elegance.

One can easily imagine a procession of elephants, the drivers on their back, swaying as they lumber along the road leading to the main entrance, the Lahore Gate, flanked by imposing, semi-octagonal towers.

We stood opposite, admiring the architecture of this stronghold, one of the characteristic monuments-symbols of Delhi. Then we made our way down Chandni Chowk avenue. Chandni Chowk, which is always crowded, is the best way to get to Old Delhi, with its winding streets, its alleyways and its innumerable markets. As if nothing has changed since the days of the Mughals, you can still see astrologers in their booths, set up on the pavements . . . reading the stars, cobblers repairing sandals, bent on their

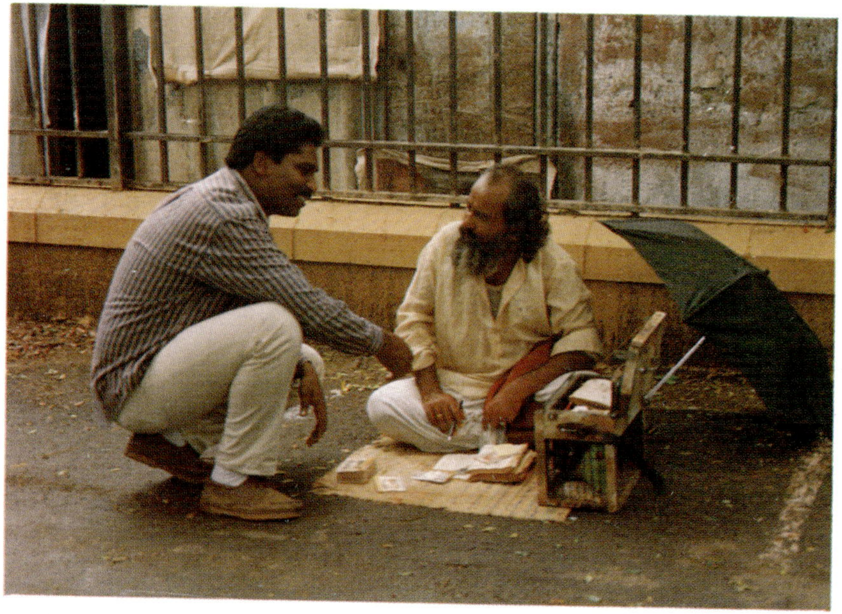

task . . . isolated from the jostling crowd and the throng all around them.

If you cast a glance inside the shanties, you see men being shaved, silver being weighed . . . and every kind of transaction you can imagine . . . while outside, the cows devour whatever they come across . . . grass, cardboard, anything edible. Strange odours fill the air, aromas from countless kinds of spices, mingled with the smell of vegetables, animal droppings and sweat. Jewellery fashioned from tiny pieces of ivory or bone, beautiful carvings, ladies' textiles, silk and cotton, are hung up outside the sheds . . . hiding their real face. There are shanties in which doctors examine the patients stoically awaiting their turn outside – in the communal waiting room.

Old Delhi is the apotheosis of Oriental glory and deception, of grandeur and squalor, of the magical and mutating Orient. Chandni Chowk and Old Delhi are places in which you can lose yourself . . . though without losing your way.

The contrast between the two cities is enormous, they are as day is to night. In one the broad, tree-lined avenues, gardens, squares, parks, huge buildings . . . and few people walking around easily, sometimes with a dog on leash . . . and in the other the asphyxiating mass . . . chock-a-block between the shanties and the animals, wandering or standing undisturbed.

This contrast, our very first impression on entering the airport in Bombay . . . accompanied us throughout our journey . . . always in its own way. Sometimes more pronounced, sometimes more discreet, to reach its climax here, on the border between Old and New Delhi, in Chandni Chowk.

It is this impression of contrast that will be with us on our return to Greece, where we shall recall and mull over the image and experiences gained in this state-continent . . . Life and death, wealth and poverty, sorrow and joy, cleanliness and filth . . . faith and indifference . . . love and hate . . . the colours whose contrast creates a synthesis . . . a hope for the conciliation of opposites . . . into the One And Unique . . . just as this city is trying to unite, essentially . . . into one.

That evening we boarded the aeroplane, to return home.